SHAHID NADEEM

Shahid Nadeem is an acclaimed Pakistani playwright who has been at the forefront of the campaign for human rights and justice in Pakistan since the late 1960s. Imprisoned by various military regimes and adopted by Amnesty International as a prisoner of conscience, he has been exiled for a period of time. When in exile in London, he worked for Amnesty International as its Campaign Coordinator and Communications Officer. Since his return to Pakistan in the late 1980s, he has served as Executive Director of Ajoka Theatre, Pakistan's leading theatre company, in which capacity he has written, directed and produced plays on a wide range of human-rights themes, including political corruption, gender violence, minority rights, peace and resistance to terrorism. He has written over forty-five plays which have been performed all over Pakistan and India. His adaptations include Brecht's *The Threepenny Opera*, *The Good Person of Szechwan*, *The Resistible Rise of Arturo Ui* and *The Caucasian Chalk Circle*. For more information about Shahid Nadeem, see page 123.

TANYA RONDER

Adaptations for theatre include *Liolà* (National Theatre); *Macbett* (RSC); *Filumena* and *Blood Wedding* (Almeida); *Peter Pan* in Kensington Gardens, 02 and US tour; *Vernon God Little* (Olivier nomination, Best New Play) and *Peribanez* (Young Vic). Original plays include *Table* (National Theatre).

DARA

adapted by
Tanya Ronder

from the play by
Shahid Nadeem

NICK HERN BOOKS
London
www.nickhernbooks.co.uk

A Nick Hern Book

This adaptation of *Dara* first published in Great Britain as a paperback original in 2015 by Nick Hern Books Limited, The Glasshouse, 49a Goldhawk Road, London W12 8QP

Adapted from the play by Shahid Nadeem, originally performed by Ajoka Theatre, Pakistan

Cover photography by Seamus Ryan; design by Graphic Design Studio at National Theatre

Designed and typeset by Nick Hern Books, London
Printed and bound in Great Britain by CPI Group (UK) Ltd

A CIP catalogue record for this book is available from the British Library

ISBN 978 1 84842 467 8

Dara at the National Theatre
Tanya Ronder

In the West we are, as a general rule, undereducated about South Asian history and also about the fastest growing religion in the world: Islam. Ajoka Theatre, in Shahid Nadeem's play *Dara*, unearthed the perfect story for us to dive into an incredible piece of Asian history and to endeavour to discover more about Islam.

In 1658, Dara, the beloved Crown Prince of the Mughal Empire, Sufi, poet, compassionate thinker, and his conservative younger brother, Aurangzeb, battled bloodily for their father's throne. Their difference of opinion about how they as Muslim rulers should deal with the vast subcontinent that was Hindustan is played out in their dramatic story.

My brief was to take Shahid Nadeem's play and adapt it for a National Theatre audience. We set out, myself and director Nadia Fall, to unpack the events cited in the original play, to educate ourselves, and to recreate the story in a way that didn't put our audience at arm's length, able to write the drama off as a story that was not theirs. The tale of Dara and Aurangzeb is one which a Pakistani or an Indian audience would have pre-existing knowledge and some ownership of. A story, albeit differently told across borders, which children all over the Indian subcontinent will have heard at school or at home, (perhaps akin to our connection in Britain to Henry VIII or Elizabeth I), but that very few of us in the West know about.

Not only is it a new story for us about a fascinating time, with a compelling cast list of people who actually existed, it is also a gift of a vehicle with which to enter into the different interpretations of Islam. Here were two brothers who had vastly contrasting understandings of this profoundly important faith. Despite a few discrepancies in source material, the core facts

explored here are indisputable; we cannot argue with them. So
these ancient events offer us the chance to dive in to the Mughal
Princes' circumstances, step into their shoes and, from that
viewpoint, strive to better understand their religious dispute.
The Sufi saying from medieval Persia – 'This too shall pass' –
serves as a wise shorthand for the perennial truth that
everything in life changes, but, fifteen hundred years after Islam
was established, the arguments over interpretation which
emerged after the death of the Prophet, peace be upon him,
reverberate today.

The National Theatre sent Nadia and myself to Pakistan and
India. We were able to see Ajoka Theatre's work in context and
visit the incredible Mughal sites of Lahore, Delhi and Agra. We
read extensively around the history of that moment. We had the
challenge of needing to imbue the play with more facts for our
audience, about both Islam and Mughal India, but also we
needed to fill out the drama. Ajoka's production was bold,
beautifully exuberant and colourful, with music and dance
central to the show, but the flavour of our theatregoing is very
different. There were more sections of reported narrative rather
than scenes, songs which have resonance in Lahore which
would fall on ignorant ears here. We needed more context, more
drama as we knew it, and less reason to detach from the tale.

In Pakistan, only Aurangzeb's story has had a generous outing
over the centuries, so Ajoka had the task of setting the record
straight by putting Dara on the map. But our task was different;
it became to ask who were both brothers as men, who were they
as children and how did the family dynamics affect their
religious beliefs and political moves?

The result is a more recognisable shape of play; it has expanded
to five acts, it starts before the original begins and ends several
decades later. I have added in a trial scene to give Dara the
voice I think we need to hear, and added various characters and
storylines, all taken from or inspired by historical facts – Itbar
and Afia, Murad, Mian Mir, Hira Bai and Aurangzeb's
relationship with her – and also incorporated a childhood for the
brothers and sisters of this Mughal court. All in an attempt to

round the story out, to make it a fairer fight between the brothers and to hopefully give our audience the psychological and emotional complexity they are used to.

Ajoka's bravery in mounting their work in current-day Pakistan, where the endeavour to question the status quo can be answered harshly, speaks for itself. The fact that Shahid Nadeem has also pinpointed so perfectly this moment in world history, which can bring us closer to an understanding of the more hidden, open and spiritual sides of Islam, is inspired. I hope that the resulting adaptation does justice, both to the original play and to the characters whose lives are depicted on stage. Especially to Dara, whose gentle, generous vision of the world never got its chance to penetrate, unfortunately for us, beyond his reach as a prince within his lifetime.

January 2015

The Original *Dara*
Shahid Nadeem

What would have been the course of Indian history had Dara Shikoh become the Emperor instead of Aurangzeb? This question has always fascinated me. The question has become more intriguing with the sharpening of the conflict between the Salafist and Sufi interpretations of Islam, and the contradictory versions of Mughal history with one side's heroes becoming the other side's villains. The Indian subcontinent has seen countless bloody power struggles, but no two contenders to the throne have been so diametrically opposed to each other.

Aurangzeb, the religious fanatic, fired with an ambition to capture power, was obsessed with the impossible dream of bringing the whole of the subcontinent under his 'Islamic' rule. He was focused, ambitious, a wily commander. He was ruthless and scheming, a manipulator par excellence, the Muslim world's answer to Machiavelli and Chanakia. On the other hand, Dara was a spoilt Crown Prince, with little battlefield experience, Emperor Shah Jahan's favourite. But he was also a poet of considerable merit, a calligraphist, a painter, a serious scholar of comparative religion and, above all, a practising Sufi, a disciple of Mian Mir and Mullah Shah Badakhshi, a close associate of the radical mystic Sarmad. While Aurangzeb wanted to bring all non-Muslim rulers to their knees, Dara wanted to search for common grounds among Indian religions. Aurangzeb was bent upon imposing a fundamentalist Sharia rule over an overwhelmingly non-Muslim India, outlawing music, poetry, fine arts. But Dara was determined to build upon Akbar's legacy of a syncretic religious and cultural ethos.

It is an extreme irony that Aurangzeb, the killer of his brothers, nephews, his own offspring, the destroyer of the Mughal Empire, has been projected as a Muslim hero, as a role model by our partisan historians and biased scholars. And Dara? He is almost non-existent. Dara, the great scholar, the sensitive artist, the passionate and devoted Sufi, the patron of arts, the prince of the people, the visionary, has almost been wiped out from the history books. Not only Dara, but Princess Jahan Ara, the amazing woman mystic and scholar, Zeb-un-Nissa Makhfi, also Aurangzeb's daughter and the great poet of the Mughal era, and Sarmad, the mysterious mystic, are all missing from our history books. If we want to reverse the retrogressive process of religious extremism and bigotry, we have to revisit this critical and dramatic point in our history.

January 2010

Shahid Nadeem's original play *Dara* was first performed by Ajoka Theatre at Alhamra Arts Council, Lahore, Pakistan, in January 2010, and later in Karachi and Islamabad in Pakistan, and Amritsar, Delhi, Lucknow, Jaipur and Hyderabad in India.

Tanya Ronder's adaptation was first performed in the Lyttelton auditorium of the National Theatre, London, on 27 January 2015 (previews from 20 January). The cast was as follows:

DARA	Zubin Varla
MALIK'S WATCHMAN	Gurjeet Singh
MALIK'S SERVANT	Scott Karim
SIPIHR	Ronak Patani
MALIK JIWAN	Emilio Doorgasingh
HIRA BAI	Anjana Vasan
AURANGZEB	Sargon Yelda
MURAD	Rudi Dharmalingam
MURAD'S AIDE	Esh Alladi
IMAD	Nicholas Khan
MASSAGE GIRL	Mariam Haque
SOLDIERS	Gary Wood, Gurjeet Singh
EMPEROR SHAH JAHAN	Vincent Ebrahim
JAHANARA	Nathalie Armin
ROSHANARA	Anneika Rose
AFIA	Anjli Mohindra
YOUNG ROSHANARA	Liya Tassisa
YOUNG JAHANARA	Mariam Haque
IMPERIAL SLAVE	Indira Joshi
ITBAR	Chook Sibtain
YOUNG AURANGZEB	Gurjeet Singh
YOUNG DARA	Ronak Patani
FAQIR	Scott Karim
DANISHMAND	Rudi Dharmalingam
MIR KHALIL	Nicholas Khan
GOVERNOR KHAN	Esh Alladi

MULLAH FAROOQ	Simon Nagra
QAZI SAYED	Emilio Doorgasingh
PROSECUTOR TALIB	Prasanna Puwanarajah
JAMAL	Gary Wood
MIAN MIR'S SECOND DISCIPLE	Nicholas Khan
AKHTAR	Gary Wood
OLD WOMAN	Indira Joshi
MIAN MIR	Ranjit Krishnamma
ITBAR'S MOTHER	Indira Joshi
ITBAR'S FATHER	Simon Nagra
EXECUTIONER	Emilio Doorgasingh
HUSSAIN	Gary Wood
PRISON GUARD	Esh Alladi
KAM	Gurjeet Singh
AZAM	Ronak Patani

All other parts played by members of the Company

Musicians	Nawazish Khan
	Kaviraj Singh Dhadyalla
	Vikaash Sankadecha

Director	Nadia Fall
Designer	Katrina Lindsay
Lighting Designer	Neil Austin
Music	Niraj Chag
Movement Director	Liam Steel
Sound Designer	Carolyn Downing
Fight Director	Kate Waters
Company Voice Work	Kate Godfrey
Vocal Music Director	Japjit Kaur
Staff Director	Ola Ince
Associate Sound Designer	Ed Ferguson
Production Consultant	Anwar Akhtar

Characters

DARA, *oldest son of Shah Jahan*
MALIK'S WATCHMAN
MALIK'S SERVANT
MALIK JIWAN, *an Afghan Chieftain*
SIPIHR, *youngest son of Dara*
AURANGZEB, *middle son of Shah Jahan*
MURAD, *youngest son of Shah Jahan*
MURAD'S AIDE
IMAD, *Aurangzeb's secretary*
MASSAGE GIRL
SOLDIER ONE, *Aurangzeb's*
SOLDIER TWO, *Aurangzeb's*
SHAH JAHAN, *Emperor*
JAHANARA, *eldest daughter of Shah Jahan*
ROSHANARA, *youngest daughter of Shah Jahan*
AFIA, *Imperial lady-in-waiting*
YOUNG AURANGZEB
YOUNG DARA
YOUNG ROSHANARA
YOUNG JAHANARA
SLAVE GIRL
IMPERIAL SLAVE
ITBAR, *Imperial eunuch*
FAQIR, *Sufi master*
DANISHMAND, *philosopher*
GOVERNOR SHAISTA KHAN, *politician*
MULLAH FAROOQ, *religious adviser*
MIR KHALIL, *Aurangzeb's cousin*
ASTROLOGER
QAZI SAYED, *court judge*
PROSECUTOR TALIB
JAMAL, *Mian Mir's first disciple*
MIAN MIR'S SECOND DISCIPLE

OLD WOMAN
MIAN MIR, *Sufi Saint*
HIRA BAI, *Hindu dancing girl*
AKHTAR, *Imperial servant*
ITBAR'S MOTHER
ITBAR'S FATHER
HUSSAIN, *Prison Warden*
PRISON GUARD
EXECUTIONER
KAM, *Aurangzeb's youngest son*
AZAM, *Aurangzeb's third son*

And SOLDIERS, SERVANTS AND SLAVES

Suggested doubling

1. DARA
2. AURANGZEB
3. SHAH JAHAN
4. JAHANARA
5. ROSHANARA
6. ITBAR
7. HIRA BAI
8. MURAD / DANISHMAND
9. FAQIR / MALIK'S SERVANT
10. MALIK JIWAN / EXECUTIONER / QAZI SAYED
11. SIPIHR / YOUNG DARA / AZAM
12. YOUNG AURANGZEB / MALIK'S WATCHMAN / KAM
13. YOUNG JAHANARA / MASSAGE GIRL
14. YOUNG ROSHANARA
15. ITBAR'S MOTHER / OLD WOMAN / PALACE SERVANT
16. MIAN MIR
17. PROSECUTOR TALIB / IMAD
18. SOLDIER ONE / HUSSAIN / AKHTAR / JAMAL, MIAN
    MIR'S FIRST DISCIPLE
19. AFIA

20. MIR KHALIL, AURANGZEB'S COUSIN / MIAN MIR'S
    SECOND DISCIPLE / SOLDIER TWO
21. GOVERNOR SHAISTA KHAN / PRISON GUARD /
    MURAD'S AIDE
22. MULLAH FAROOQ / ITBAR'S FATHER

COMPANY: SOLDIERS, SERVANTS, SLAVES

MUSICIANS

This text went to press before the end of rehearsals and so may differ slightly from the play as performed.

ACT ONE

Scene One

DARA (*forty-four*), *in a thin linen tunic, bangs on a huge door. He is half-wild with hunger and exhaustion. It is early 1659, Mughal India.*

WATCHMAN. Who's there?

DARA. Open up.

WATCHMAN. Announce yourself, sir.

DARA. Fetch your master.

The WATCHMAN *opens a hatch in the door, peers out.*

WATCHMAN. Your name, sir?

Silence.

I can't hear, you have to shout through this wood, it's such a heavy door.

The WATCHMAN *speaks to another* SERVANT *inside.*

He won't give his name.

SERVANT. Why not?

WATCHMAN. I don't know.

SERVANT (*to* DARA, *through the door*). Can you tell us who you are, sir?

DARA. Malik Jiwan will know, I am no foe, fetch him.

SERVANT. We can't, sir, without your name.

DARA. Open, will you.

WATCHMAN. If we can just take your –

DARA (*snaps*). I am not giving it to you, get your master!

SIPIHR, *a boy of thirteen, joins* DARA.

Without the usual pageant, they want my name. I should have given it, they're not to know it's all I have.

Almost laughing at the absurdity of his situation.

Pushing me to pass it through some commonplace door.

SIPIHR. Father…

DARA. Even releasing a lock seems beyond me these days.

SIPIHR. Let's ride on, it's half a day to Persia…

DARA. I know where we are. We need help.

SIPIHR. Food?

They are both hungry.

DARA. Not just food. Malik has gold to give, Sipihr. We cannot turn up as beggars in Persia, stinking of defeat. They're friends, yes, but still, we need a rock, a foundation, upon which to build the new army.

SIPIHR. You trust Malik?

DARA. I saved his life, Sipihr.

SIPIHR. But is he trustworthy?

DARA. What are we jeopardising? There is nothing left to take.

SIPIHR. There is you that is left to take.

DARA *responds more gently.*

DARA. We could all be taken at any moment, whenever Allah sees fit. We have no choice, we have to stop Aurangzeb, Sipihr, or our Empire will petrify. He is a blinkered bigot, a narrower vision of Islam never existed, we will all be driven underground.

MALIK *speaks through the door,* SIPIHR *steps back.*

MALIK. Who's there?

DARA. Malik Jiwan?

MALIK. What do you want?

DARA. A harmonious kingdom, a glass of water…? It's a difficult question to answer.

The door creaks open.

I know how I must look.

MALIK. Is that Prince Dara?

DARA. Emperor Dara, according to my father, but… he is imprisoned in his own palace. I am Shah Jahan's Crown Prince.

A sudden movement, SIPIHR *emerges from the shadows,* MALIK *slams the door.*

MALIK. Defend!

MALIK*'s* MEN *position themselves, armed, behind the door.* DARA *shouts to be heard.*

DARA. It's my son, Malik Jiwan, my son, Sipihr!

Slowly the door opens again. DARA *ushers* SIPIHR *forwards.*

The bravest of youths… His current garb does not represent his qualities but, which exterior was ever eloquent about the pearl within?

SIPIHR. Greetings, Sir Jiwan.

MALIK. Where are your men?

DARA. All in all we are thirty.

MALIK. Thirty?

DARA. The best thirty, the apostles of loyalty. A month ago we were a thousand times that many but, now, are without military escort.

MALIK. Who drives you to this, Prince Dara?

DARA. My brother, Malik Jiwan.

MALIK. Prince Aurangzeb?

DARA. The same. He has Delhi, and he has Agra Fort surrounded, my father and sister, Jahanara, beyond my care's reach, inside. He uses my home for his family whilst his fast-swelling army hunts us down, baby brother Murad in tow. Aurangzeb claims no interest in the throne, yet he craves it unreservedly, but our father, the Emperor, still lives so I will not let him have it.

MALIK. You have always been brave, Prince Dara.

DARA. It's bluster, Malik Jiwan – part grief, part fear, mostly fury. I am gripped with hatred for Aurangzeb as I have never been for anyone.

MALIK. Allah tests you, Prince.

DARA. And I am ready. We need a night or two under your roof before we march through the Bolan Pass to regroup. We might have reached Persia weeks ago if my wife –

He breaks off.

MALIK. Your beloved princess?

SIPIHR *steps in to save* DARA*'s emotion from rising.*

SIPIHR. The remainder of our army returned to Lahore with my mother's body.

MALIK. Allah, may she rest in peace…

SIPIHR. They buried her next to her Sufi master, Mian Mir's tomb.

DARA. Digging in the dark like thieves, because we are Aurangzeb's enemies now, no Sufi is safe.

MALIK. I'm sorry.

DARA. In Ajmer, while we battled, they ransacked our women. The men we paid to guard them took everything – the clothes, the carriages – all they left was the tent in which Nadira relinquished her life. She had no stomach for war. The less one has the closer one is to God, yet this death punches the bliss from me. But here you are at the edge of our Empire.

MALIK. And here we stand talking in the dark. Come in, Prince, you are welcome, welcome.

DARA. Thank you, Malik Jiwan.

MALIK. I'd not be here were it not for you, Prince, I'd have been crunched under your father's formidable elephant.

DARA *laughs with relief,* MALIK *joins his laughter.*

DARA. Please, let us follow you in.

Scene Two

AURANGZEB *(forty-two) carefully unfolds a prayer mat. A* MUEZZIN *sings the call to prayer (this could be* SHAH JAHAN). *In the gaps of song,* HIRA BAI, *a girl in another time, another place – a memory of* AURANGZEB*'s – sings a Hindu song.* AURANGZEB *prays. He is in a large tent pitched amongst his army.* HIRA BAI *sings again;* AURANGZEB, *distracted by her, turns to look. His attention is snapped back by* MURAD *appearing at the entrance to his tent, his* AIDE *behind him.* AURANGZEB *completes his prayers, rolls up his mat, greets* MURAD *warmly.*

AURANGZEB. Brother.

MURAD. Aurangzeb.

AURANGZEB. I'm glad you came, please join me.

MURAD *doesn't.*

My man will fetch your man some tea.

AURANGZEB *points outside the tent.*

MURAD. He stays.

AURANGZEB. Then we shall have tea brought.

The AIDE *stands by the entrance.*

And wine for you, Murad?

Beat.

MURAD. Are you drinking?

AURANGZEB. We must celebrate, Your Highness…

MURAD. How, Your Holiness? You never indulge.

AURANGZEB. In alcohol, no.

MURAD. I like wine more than almost everything.

IMAD, AURANGZEB*'s secretary, brings* MURAD *the drinks.*

AURANGZEB. I brought an excellent crate for you, brother.

MURAD. How do you know it's excellent? You must sometimes want the taste in your mouth?

AURANGZEB. Not at all.

MURAD. Did you ever sip it even?

AURANGZEB. No.

MURAD. I could drink all day long.

MURAD *drinks, watching* AURANGZEB.

Was it Grandfather Jahangir who put you off?

AURANGZEB. I don't need a human spectre.

MURAD. Just the cautions of the Quran. 'Two lips, one for drinking, the other for apologising' – know who said that?

AURANGZEB. Grandfather, frequently.

MURAD. When he diluted his rum to slow his decay, he thinned it not with water, as a wise man would, but with wine, confirming that alcohol weakens the intellect. Not as much as opium, admittedly, which Grandfather was famously also partial to but, you saw all that.

AURANGZEB. I don't remember much.

MURAD. Finished imbibing by late morning, was fast asleep by lunch, propped up on cushions like a whore. He drank, his wife ruled. You lived there two whole years.

AURANGZEB. I was a child, they weren't important times.

MURAD. Oh, so everything before Father was Emperor is irrelevant?

AURANGZEB. No.

MURAD. I don't remember it anyway.

AURANGZEB. You were an infant. Is the wine good, would you like more?

MURAD *finally says what he's been getting at.*

MURAD. Why don't you mind that I drink?

AURANGZEB. Because you're a soldier to the core, that's who you are. They don't understand you at Court, they haven't grasped that the worm turned long ago.

MURAD. I don't need your protection, Aurangzeb, I know what they say and I know what they'll be thinking when they bow to me.

AURANGZEB. They need to look in your eyes to see the boldness.

MURAD. My Timur blood.

AURANGZEB. Stronger in you, Murad, than in the rest of us put together.

MURAD. It's worth remembering that, Aurangzeb.

AURANGZEB. More?

AURANGZEB *pours wine.*

MURAD. Why did you rush ahead?

AURANGZEB. Why did you stay behind?

MURAD. You – (*Continuing his next speech, fighting to be heard over* AURANGZEB.)

AURANGZEB (*overlapping*). The astrologers said it was auspicious to forge forwards, we had to respond quickly –

MURAD (*overlapping*). You made me question our arrangement. We were fighting side by side and suddenly, without warning, my men were at the back like sheep.

AURANGZEB. I am impatient to deliver you to Delhi, brother, to have your name emblazoned on the coins. You got my letters?

MURAD (*still suspicious*). I got three.

AURANGZEB. Murad, you are perfectly ripe, the Indian Empire, all of Hindustan, is thirsty for this change.

MURAD *cuts to the chase.*

MURAD. Why not you, what stops you from ruling?

AURANGZEB. I am not a king. But whilst I wish my brother well I will not sit back and watch Dara take the throne.

MURAD. Because he would dissipate our religion?

AURANGZEB. Dilute and dissipate, his religious observance is lax.

MURAD. And mine is not?

AURANGZEB. You do not spend your days writing mystical poetry.

MURAD *can't help but smirk.*

MURAD. His soldiering is lax too.

He indicates himself and AURANGZEB.

We two were sent out to wrestle our corner, and look what we've both built up! I know how to lead, like our Timurid ancestors. They may have looked pallid, with their lily skin and green eyes, but, brother, they were ferocious, and covered continents to conquer. Being closeted in the fort, Dara imagines everyone springs from the same happy fount.

AURANGZEB. He melds.

MURAD. Did you see his soldiers? That wasn't an army, it was a collection of bakers and cobblers with swords. Do you know, when he writes, he still addresses me as baby brother?

AURANGZEB. I serve my Empire by placing an Emperor I believe in on the Peacock Throne. Then show me a room and let me devour the words of Allah and his Prophet, may peace be upon him, for the rest of my days.

MURAD *finds it difficult to believe*.

MURAD. Where do you envisage this room being?

AURANGZEB. Wherever you see fit, Your Highness. I trust you, brother, I serve you well in this war.

MURAD *helps himself to wine*.

MURAD. The people of Delhi adore Dara.

AURANGZEB. He throws them money, of course they love him.

MURAD. Can I trust *you*, Aurangzeb?

AURANGZEB. As God is my witness.

MURAD. Where's your holy book?

AURANGZEB. Here.

He brings out his Quran.

MURAD. I thought you memorised it long ago?

AURANGZEB. Still, it is always with me.

MURAD. Swear on it.

AURANGZEB. Swear what?

MURAD. What you will.

AURANGZEB *places his hand on the Quran*.

AURANGZEB. I swear that I am working, in your best interests, to deliver what our Empire most needs. You at its helm.

MURAD *indicates the Quran*.

MURAD. You wouldn't spit on that in a hurry.

AURANGZEB *hides his disgust at* MURAD*'s disrespectful language.*

AURANGZEB. Why don't you stay? I can offer the massage services of an expert slave girl.

MURAD. Is she good?

AURANGZEB. Very. My tent is yours, brother, anything you need.

A GIRL *comes in.*

MASSAGE GIRL. May I remove your boots, sir?

AURANGZEB (*to* MURAD'S AIDE). He's perfectly safe.

AIDE. I'll stay if you don't mind, sir.

AURANGZEB. Of course. (*To* MURAD.) Sleep well, Your Highness.

MURAD, *giving himself over to his massage, expels a sound of deep satisfaction.* AURANGZEB *leaves.*

Scene Three

DARA *and* SIPIHR *emerge, clean and rested.* MALIK *is with them.*

DARA. I cannot thank you enough, Malik Jiwan.

SIPIHR. Allah be with you, sir.

MALIK. Gather a strong army, may your desires come true.

DARA. They will, Malik, on the back of your charity. We already had him, nearly, at Samugarh, thanks to Sipihr.

MALIK (*to* SIPIHR). See your father's pride?

DARA. This one galloped his whole ten thousand into Aurangzeb's flanks and broke them.

MALIK. Good boy.

DARA. Then in a second of confusion, my general urged me down from my elephant. 'You'll be nimbler on a horse!', he shouts. My soldiers, seeing my empty howdah, think I've been killed. That moment, Aurangzeb sounds the victory drum so my soldiers panic. A hot wind picked up and the day turned. Do you know what Aurangzeb had done?

MALIK. No.

DARA. Paid my loyal general a hundred thousand rupees to get me down from my howdah.

MALIK. That is underhand.

DARA. That is Aurangzeb's warfare.

MALIK. Next time, Dara, may the day be yours.

A storm of SOLDIERS *arrives.*

DARA. Sipihr, run, we are betrayed, run, boy, run!

SIPIHR *escapes,* SOLDIERS *grab* DARA.

MALIK. After him, quickly.

Two SOLDIERS *follow* SIPIHR, *shouting.*

SOLDIER ONE. Go that way, get him!

SOLDIER TWO. I am!

DARA. Never stop running, Sipihr!

He turns to MALIK.

Is this the colour of your gratitude, peddling me to my brother as soon as I'm past your walls?

MALIK. Forgive me, Prince, it is unsafe to be on the loser's side.

DARA. You are the loser, Malik. With a heart that corrupt, what hope is there for your soul?

DARA *is marched off.*

Scene Four

AURANGZEB*'s tent.* MURAD *sleeps.* AURANGZEB *appears. He whispers.*

AURANGZEB. Officer?

MURAD'S AIDE *is sleepy but awake.*

AIDE. Sir?

AURANGZEB. I need some advice.

The AIDE *is flattered.*

A visitor came looking for your master, come tell me if you know him.

As soon as the AIDE *steps outside, he is garrotted by* AURANGZEB*'s* MEN. *Two more* MEN *come for* MURAD. *Quietly, they remove his weapons and lock his feet together.* MURAD *wakes.*

MURAD. What are you doing? Not this, no, no... Aurangzeb!

There is a struggle.

AURANGZEB. The fetters are golden, Murad. It is for your own benefit.

MURAD. You swore on the Quran!

AURANGZEB. Small deceits are sometimes necessary –

MURAD (*interrupting*). Liar!

AURANGZEB (*continuing*). – in order to fortify Islam.

MURAD. Where are my men?

AURANGZEB. He was the last. The rest are on my payroll already, baby brother.

Scene Five

In Agra Fort, SHAH JAHAN *rails against a letter.*

JAHANARA. Is he coming here?

SHAH JAHAN. Aurangzeb hasn't the decency to face me, sending me orders from Delhi! Incompetent to rule, how dare he? I'd sooner grind my pearls to dust than give them to him.

He wears a string of enormous pearls.

Common property indeed!

JAHANARA. He wants it all, Baba, your place on the throne and everything that goes with it.

SHAH JAHAN. I am not finished yet, and when the time comes, I have chosen my successor.

JAHANARA. You know it never unfolds like that, Baba, every one of your sons is a contender.

SHAH JAHAN. What are you saying, Jahanara, I should have killed the others off?

JAHANARA. No, Baba, but this war, all those lives… it's insatiable. To secure Dara as Emperor, the others needed to be managed, somehow.

SHAH JAHAN. Without bloodshed, how?

JAHANARA *can't answer.*

What can we do from here?

JAHANARA. Wait, is all. As ever.

SHAH JAHAN. Until Dara returns to march on Aurangzeb.

JAHANARA. We don't even know where Dara is, he may be months away, how can we know?

SHAH JAHAN. The little white snake, it's not enough to have me trapped here like a bear, Aurangzeb wants my fort, he knows the jewels I have in my cellars.

JAHANARA. Stop it, Baba, what can you offer? Send Aurangzeb something, create time for us to think.

SHAH JAHAN. A glass of poison, humanity in his soul? Look what he is doing to me!

JAHANARA. And what did you do to your own kin when you were in Aurangzeb's position, your surviving brother, your nephews and cousins? Family blood had not been shed on accession before you, Baba.

SHAH JAHAN *is sobered by this*.

What about your sword?

SHAH JAHAN. Alamgir, you mean Alamgir?

JAHANARA. Yes, Alamgir, that would please him.

SHAH JAHAN. It is a sword built for an Emperor, it is mine!

JAHANARA. I know, Baba, but we have to work with him, not against him.

SHAH JAHAN. What if Dara comes?

JAHANARA. Then everything would change.

Beat.

SHAH JAHAN. I need a girl, fetch me a girl, Jahanara.

JAHANARA. Which one?

SHAH JAHAN. You choose, sweetmeats are tasty whichever stall they're from.

JAHANARA. It's not good for you, Baba, it's a stress on your body.

SHAH JAHAN. So give me more silver oil, more crocodile eggs, to keep me virile, I am a loving man, Jahanara.

JAHANARA. I know, Baba, the most loving, but you are getting old.

SHAH JAHAN. Not old, not yet, I am not done yet.

Scene Six

Red Fort, Delhi. AURANGZEB *is presented with Alamgir.*

ROSHANARA. A sword?

AURANGZEB. The blade he's always used.

ROSHANARA. The one we weren't allowed to touch as children?

AURANGZEB. You can touch it now.

ROSHANARA. May I hold it?

AURANGZEB. Yes, but don't drop it.

ROSHANARA. I won't, Seizer of the Universe.

AURANGZEB. Stop it, Roshanara.

She laughs.

What's funny? That is the sword's name, not mine.

ROSHANARA. But it will be yours. Murad is captured, Dara is captured, Father is confined.

AURANGZEB *tries to laugh too.*

What does he want?

AURANGZEB. He's buying time for Dara, as ever.

ROSHANARA. Then he's spending money in an empty shop.

IMAD *enters, bows deeply.*

IMAD. My lord, Prince Dara is a day away.

AURANGZEB. Fine, good. Imad?

IMAD. Yes, Sire.

AURANGZEB. Before they enter Delhi, they must change elephants.

IMAD. Yes, Sire.

AURANGZEB. You know Babita?

IMAD. Babita is sick, Sire.

AURANGZEB. So I hear. I want Dara to ride in on that elephant, just as she is. And Sipihr?

IMAD. No news as yet, Sire.

AURANGZEB. Once Dara is here, I will watch from the upper walls.

IMAD *nods and goes*. ROSHANARA *hands back the sword*.

ROSHANARA. What must Dara be thinking?

AURANGZEB. He deserves every thought. Humiliation is new to him, he's still sticky with our mother's milk.

ROSHANARA. Father should watch, and Jahanara, can't you bring them from Agra?

AURANGZEB. I do not have access to them yet. And anyway, his days of appearing in public are over.

ROSHANARA. So Father will end his days in a fort the size of a walled city?

AURANGZEB. In the harem of Agra Fort, I will limit him to that section as soon as we can –

ROSHANARA *interrupts* AURANGZEB *with a laugh*.

ROSHANARA. The women's quarters, how fitting!

AURANGZEB. Roshanara, you need to control yourself, it is not apposite to interrupt an Emperor.

ROSHANARA. I'm sorry, Your Highness.

AURANGZEB. Allow me to offer you some wisdom – the key to conquering the self lies in restraint.

ROSHANARA. I apologise, please continue.

AURANGZEB. My plan is to lock Father in his own harem as soon as we gain entry.

ROSHANARA. Why don't you just attack, go in?

AURANGZEB. And destroy those towering walls, which are now mine?

ROSHANARA. You need him to surrender, beg for mercy.

AURANGZEB. Once he has realised he cannot hold the fort for ever...

ROSHANARA. But that could take months! How much food do they have?

AURANGZEB. The kitchens are full.

ROSHANARA. So as long as they have water and enough to eat...

An idea arises for AURANGZEB.

What? Oh.

He summons IMAD.

AURANGZEB. Imad? Fetch Shaista Khan.

IMAD *bows and leaves.* ROSHANARA *understands* AURANGZEB*'s thinking.*

ROSHANARA. You can drive them out with thirst.

In a flow of water we catch a snatch of HIRA BAI *learning how to wash before prayer.* AURANGZEB *is caught by the memory.*

HIRA BAI. Three times...

She washes her hands.

Swish and spit.

She swishes and spits.

Three times.

HIRA BAI *is mischievous, squirts the water sideways at someone. The flow of water suddenly stops.*

Scene Seven

In Agra, JAHANARA *interrogates* AFIA, *an Imperial lady-in-waiting.*

JAHANARA. The pipes cannot all be empty, try the bathing rooms again!

AFIA. They're dry, my lady, all of them, dry.

JAHANARA. Everything is lost if there is no water, we cannot cook, we cannot drink, we cannot pray!

AFIA. Emperor Aurangzeb must know this, my lady.

JAHANARA. How could he? Are you not scared to die, Afia?

AFIA. Not yet, my lady.

JAHANARA. Why?

AFIA. Because I trust that you will leave the fort and beg your brother, on your father's behalf, for water.

JAHANARA. What else can I do, Afia?

AFIA. I think Emperor Aurangzeb must know this too, my lady. He understands you have no option.

JAHANARA. Your deaths would be on my hands – my father's, yours, your children's… of course I must go begging. I know he knows, he has us all now.

ACT TWO

Scene One

The past.

JAHANARA *gives way to her younger self,* YOUNG
JAHANARA *(fourteen). She is joined by* YOUNG
ROSHANARA *(eleven). It is thirty years earlier, 1629, the Red
Fort, Delhi. There is drumming from the Drum Room. A* SLAVE
GIRL *sweeps the great hall with a brush of branches, a* MALE
SERVANT, *squatting, cleans between the floor tiles. Swallows
swoop and twitter through the open hall. An* IMPERIAL
SLAVE *rushes through. The girls follow. She stops them.*

IMPERIAL SLAVE. Not yet.

She goes.

YOUNG ROSHANARA. She just has baby after baby.

YOUNG JAHANARA. They are your brothers and sisters,
Roshanara.

YOUNG ROSHANARA. Each one makes her weaker, even
when the baby doesn't live!

YOUNG JAHANARA. What do you suggest, she stops having
children?

YOUNG ROSHANARA. There are enough of us already,
aren't there?

YOUNG JAHANARA. Roshanara!

YOUNG ROSHANARA. You know what's going to happen if
she dies, don't you?

YOUNG JAHANARA. I can't believe you just said that.

YOUNG ROSHANARA. Everybody dies, even Emperor's wives.

YOUNG JAHANARA. You need to be quiet.

YOUNG ROSHANARA. You'll be in charge, First Lady of the Empire, you'll make all the decisions and everyone will forget about me.

YOUNG JAHANARA. Don't talk to me when you're in this mood.

YOUNG ROSHANARA *plumps herself down on a large cushion.*

I was going to sit there, I'm tired.

YOUNG ROSHANARA. Go to sleep then.

YOUNG ROSHANARA *moves.*

YOUNG JAHANARA. I wish they'd bring news.

YOUNG ROSHANARA. It's probably another girl. Why are you smiling?

YOUNG JAHANARA. Because babies are adorable. Not like you, grumpy, what's the matter?

YOUNG ROSHANARA. I'm bored!

YOUNG JAHANARA. Shall I call the tutor, ask for more lessons?

YOUNG ROSHANARA. No!

YOUNG JAHANARA. Get your sewing out.

YOUNG ROSHANARA. I don't want to sew!

YOUNG JAHANARA. It always feels this way when we have to wait.

YOUNG ROSHANARA. It wouldn't if we were boys.

YOUNG JAHANARA. What would you do if you were a boy?

YOUNG ROSHANARA. Go outside, run, fight.

YOUNG JAHANARA. Would you? You know what I'd do?

YOUNG ROSHANARA. Sew cushions?

YOUNG JAHANARA. I'd marry.

YOUNG ROSHANARA. Do you want to get married?

YOUNG JAHANARA. Sometimes.

YOUNG ROSHANARA. And have children?

YOUNG JAHANARA. Yes.

YOUNG ROSHANARA. I'm glad we can't. If you have boys they grow up more powerful than you, with girls they end up hating you.

YOUNG JAHANARA. I don't hate Ami!

YOUNG ROSHANARA. Have you met someone?

YOUNG JAHANARA. Where? We never get the chance. Though that might change when Dara is Emperor. Have you?

YOUNG ROSHANARA. What?

YOUNG JAHANARA. Met someone?

YOUNG ROSHANARA *looks away.*

I don't believe it, Roshanara, how, you're eleven years old?

YOUNG ROSHANARA. You're fourteen, catch up.

ITBAR, *a eunuch, comes in with an infant's jacket.*

Girl's talk, Itbar.

ITBAR. Am I not a girl?

YOUNG ROSHANARA. Well, you're a eunuch...

YOUNG JAHANARA. Do you want to be a girl?

ITBAR. Not really.

YOUNG JAHANARA *jokes with* ITBAR, *they are easy and familiar.*

YOUNG JAHANARA. Well then, you're a man and can't join our conversation!

The boys run in. As they pass the water, YOUNG DARA *(thirteen) splashes* YOUNG AURANGZEB *(eleven).*

YOUNG AURANGZEB. Don't, Dara!

YOUNG DARA. What did I do?

YOUNG AURANGZEB *(to* ITBAR*).* He splashed me!

ITBAR. Calm down, boys.

YOUNG AURANGZEB *shows his wet patches.*

YOUNG AURANGZEB. Look. *(To* DARA.*)* You always do this when Father's coming.

DARA. You're always so serious when Father's coming.

YOUNG AURANGZEB. No, I'm not!

YOUNG ROSHANARA *splashes* YOUNG DARA. *He, in good humour, splashes her back.*

YOUNG ROSHANARA. Ah, you soaked me!

YOUNG DARA. I'm a better aim than you. Would you like my jacket?

YOUNG ROSHANARA. No, because then I'll look like a boy.

YOUNG DARA *points to the jacket* ITBAR *is holding.*

YOUNG DARA. Take Murad's, wear your baby brother's jacket!

YOUNG AURANGZEB. Would you like mine, Roshanara?

YOUNG ROSHANARA *doesn't listen, she splashes* YOUNG DARA *again.*

ITBAR. Roshanara!

YOUNG ROSHANARA. What?

YOUNG DARA *and* YOUNG ROSHANARA *laugh,* YOUNG AURANGZEB *is deadly serious.* SHAH JAHAN *enters. The girls run to him, anxious for news.*

SHAH JAHAN. Gather round.

YOUNG JAHANARA. Baba?

YOUNG ROSHANARA. What's happened, Father?

SHAH JAHAN. We have a song to prepare, all the way from France, it's for your mother. Who can tell me where France is?

YOUNG DARA. It's close to that little island…

YOUNG JAHANARA. The British Isles.

SHAH JAHAN. And the monarch?

YOUNG JAHANARA. King Charles.

SHAH JAHAN. No, petal, he rules the little isles, who rules France?

A SERVANT *enters,* SHAH JAHAN *looks at him.*

SERVANT. Excuse me, Your Excellency, a faqir is here.

SHAH JAHAN. Did he bring anything with him?

SERVANT. He did, Sire, he is carrying fruit.

SHAH JAHAN. What kind of fruit?

SERVANT. Apples, Sire.

SHAH JAHAN. Then show him in.

The SERVANT *goes out backwards, never turning his back on the Emperor. The girls cover their faces with veils.*

King Louis the XIII.

YOUNG DARA. Ah, Louis the Just!

The SERVANT *returns with a young* FAQIR *with long uncovered hair and very little on. He holds apples.*

SHAH JAHAN. Two red apples. How?

FAQIR. Trees, my lord.

SHAH JAHAN. Which trees?

FAQIR. They are invisible to some eyes.

SHAH JAHAN. If there's one thing I've learnt as Emperor it's to disregard a pregnant lady's wishes at your peril. My wife yearns for apples. I've had every tree in Kashmir investigated, the entire region, nothing is in season, and yet you arrive with two shiny apples.

He takes the apples.

Where is your tree?

FAQIR. Oh, it is not my tree, Sire.

He giggles.

I possess nothing but what you see me in.

SHAH JAHAN. Yet you bring more than gold.

FAQIR. I'm glad. May I ask you a question, Sire?

SHAH JAHAN. Go on.

FAQIR. Smell your hands.

SHAH JAHAN *sniffs his palms.*

What do they smell of?

SHAH JAHAN. Apples, the distinct smell of these beautiful fruits.

FAQIR. Whenever you suffer ill-health, Sire, inhale the odour from your hands. If you still smell the scent of apples, you have longer to live, when you cease to smell apples, your life has reached its term.

There is a shift of tone for SHAH JAHAN, *he now takes this* FAQIR *very seriously.*

SHAH JAHAN. Will it be sickness, Faqir, will I die a natural death?

FAQIR. I cannot tell that, Sire, I only see what I see.

SHAH JAHAN. Which is more than you say. I charge you, a question, which son of mine, born or unborn, will destroy my bloodline?

FAQIR. I'm sorry, Sire?

SHAH JAHAN. Answer.

FAQIR. That is unfair to ask, Sire, and with two of your sons present...

SHAH JAHAN. Nonetheless, it is the question I pose.

FAQIR. They are just boys.

SHAH JAHAN. They are princes, princes have ears of flint, answer the question, I command you.

FAQIR. What if I were wrong, Sire?

SHAH JAHAN. You could lie to me or you could tell me what you see, but if you do neither you will not live beyond sundown.

FAQIR. The middle of your living sons, the one with pale skin.

SHAH JAHAN. Aurangzeb?

The children look at each other.

FAQIR. I beg you, Sire, please don't...

SHAH JAHAN. Come here, Aurangzeb.

YOUNG AURANGZEB *steps forward.*

Did you hear what this Faqir said?

YOUNG AURANGZEB. Yes, Father.

SHAH JAHAN. Are you going to destroy me one day, boy, well?

YOUNG AURANGZEB. No, Father.

SHAH JAHAN. You had better not, you little snake, do you hear?

YOUNG JAHANARA *tries to break the intensity.*

YOUNG JAHANARA. Why would he, Father?

YOUNG AURANGZEB. Why would I?

SHAH JAHAN. You better had not.

(*To a* SERVANT.) Take these apples to my wife, give them to her ladies, run.

The SERVANT *bows, takes the apples and leaves, running backwards.* SHAH JAHAN *smells his hands.*

I have always counted on the planets, my court astrologers, for glimpses of the future, but here I am told my fortune by a Muslim miracle-worker, a Sufi faqir, an all-seeing mendicant.

FAQIR. Not that, Sire...

SHAH JAHAN. I don't know what sort of magic it is you practise, but I am grateful.

FAQIR. No magic, your lordship, I didn't mean to misguide you. I follow the Prophet's, may peace be upon him, path of love, a road which continually sheds light on what we see and on our destinies.

He speaks mainly for YOUNG AURANGZEB.

Every one of us, within Allah's measure, can open our fate up, like a flower, lift up to the sun and broaden our way.

SHAH JAHAN (*to* FAQIR). Don't leave without filling your purse.

FAQIR. I have no need of money, Sire.

SHAH JAHAN. No? Food, then.

FAQIR. Nor food, Sire, thank you.

SHAH JAHAN (*to* SERVANT). He wants for nothing, show him out.

FAQIR. Goodbye, children of the Empire, forgive my imprudence. Remember that rock is the same as a jewel, the only difference being, the latter holds light.

The FAQIR *leaves with* SERVANT, *backwards.*

YOUNG DARA. Who was he, Father, who was that faqir?

SHAH JAHAN. I met him on the mosque steps.

YOUNG DARA. How can Sufis see like that?

YOUNG AURANGZEB. See what?

YOUNG DARA. Everything.

YOUNG AURANGZEB. They see nothing, nothing!

YOUNG ROSHANARA. How can he be a Muslim, Baba, he didn't even have clothes on?

YOUNG AURANGZEB. He's not a real Muslim.

YOUNG DARA. Clothes are irrelevant.

YOUNG AURANGZEB. Not in the Quran!

YOUNG JAHANARA. It's a different kind of Muslim.

YOUNG DARA. I'd rather that than the Mullah's long cloaks.

SHAH JAHAN. 'The best garment is the garment of righteousness.'

YOUNG DARA *proves his point to* YOUNG AURANGZEB.

YOUNG DARA. See? The Quran.

SHAH JAHAN. This is King Louis's favourite song, about the birth of a child, ready?

ALL THE CHILDREN. Yes, Father.

SHAH JAHAN (*singing*).
    D'où viens-tu, bergère?
    D'où viens-tu?

With me, go.

They all step forward to learn the song.

SHAH JAHAN *and* CHILDREN (*singing*).
    D'où viens-tu, bergère?
    D'où viens-tu?

SHAH JAHAN (*singing*).
    Je viens de l'étable,
    De m'y promener.

SHAH JAHAN *and* CHILDREN (*singing*).
> *Je viens de l'étable,*
> *De m'y promener.*

SHAH JAHAN (*singing*).
> *J'ai vu un miracle*
> *Ce soir arrivé.*

SHAH JAHAN *and* CHILDREN (*singing*).
> *J'ai vu un miracle*
> *Ce soir arrivé.*

He sets up a simple dance step for them to do as they sing.

SHAH JAHAN (*singing*).
> *Qu'as-tu vu, bergère?*
> *Qu'as-tu vu?*   .

They all sing and do the dance step. ITBAR *joins in, making* MURAD*'s jacket dance.*

SHAH JAHAN *and* CHILDREN (*singing*).
> *Qu'as-tu vu, bergère?*
> *Qu'as-tu vu?*

SHAH JAHAN. Step back, Aurangzeb.

YOUNG AURANGZEB *looks confused.*

You're out of time.

(*Singing.*)
> *J'ai vu dans la crèche*
> *Un petit enfant.*

Singing and stepping.

SHAH JAHAN *and* CHILDREN.
> *J'ai vu dans la crèche*
> *Un petit enfant.*

SHAH JAHAN (*to* ITBAR). Take him to the courtyard or, wherever his baby brother is.

ITBAR. Yes, Sire.

YOUNG AURANGZEB *is devastated.* ITBAR *takes* YOUNG AURANGZEB *off.*

SHAH JAHAN *(singing).*
    Sur le paille fraîche
    Mis bien tendrement.

The others sing, but YOUNG ROSHANARA *drops out.*

SHAH JAHAN *and* CHILDREN *(singing).*
    Sur le paille fraîche
    Mis bien tendrement.

YOUNG ROSHANARA *runs out after* YOUNG AURANGZEB.

YOUNG ROSHANARA. Aurangzeb?

(Shouting back into the room.) He's not a snake, you're all snakes!

YOUNG DARA. Aurangzeb?

YOUNG DARA *and* YOUNG JAHANARA *are left.*

SHAH JAHAN. Ignore them, once again from the top.

SHAH JAHAN, YOUNG DARA *and* YOUNG JAHANARA *(singing).*
    D'où viens-tu, bergère?
    D'où viens-tu?

SHAH JAHAN. On your own.

YOUNG DARA *and* YOUNG JAHANARA *(singing).*
    D'où viens-tu, bergère?
    D'où viens-tu?

SHAH JAHAN, YOUNG DARA *and* YOUNG JAHANARA *(singing).*
    Je viens de l'étable,
    De m'y promener.

SHAH JAHAN. You have a fine voice, Dara, firm but soft within, like a watermelon, my watermelon!

(*To* YOUNG JAHANARA.) And you, my petal, are a fresh spring.

SHAH JAHAN, YOUNG DARA *and* YOUNG JAHANARA (*singing*).
> *J'ai vu un miracle*
> *Ce soir arrivé.*
> *Qu'as-tu vu, bergère?*
> *Qu'as-tu vu?*
> *Qu'as-tu vu, bergère?*
> *Qu'as-tu vu?*

Scene Two

The past.

A burst of flames. Fifteen years later, 1644. YOUNG JAHANARA *gives way to* JAHANARA, *who is bundled off.* ITBAR *and the* FAQIR *are mid-thirties, speaking in hushed, hurried tones.*

FAQIR. It was a lamp which set the Princess alight?

ITBAR. In the passageway, it wasn't properly in its alcove, her dress and hijab went up like kindling. Two slave girls died trying to smother the flames.

FAQIR. Poor children.

ITBAR. The Emperor throws doctor after doctor at her, local, foreign, now you.

FAQIR. If I can be of any service…

ITBAR. Princess Jahanara will live or die, we cannot influence which, it's Shah Jahan who needs help. Losing his wife, Mumtaz, nearly slew him, were Jahanara to go too he would crawl to his grave. He mews like a kitten by her side. His children are gathering, young Murad arrived from the Punjab last night.

FAQIR. Is Aurangzeb…?

ITBAR. Not here yet. Dara has been at her bedside, along with their father, since the accident. No apples today?

FAQIR. There was no request for fruit.

ITBAR. Next time you're summoned, in another fifteen years, His Majesty's favourite is watermelon and he's partial to a mango.

FAQIR. How quickly fifteen years passes.

ITBAR. Let's go.

They head off. ITBAR *speaks as they leave.*

Just to warn you, her wounds go through muscle and fat to bone, her left arm is under question – should they or shouldn't they amputate?

ROSHANARA (*twenty-six*) *hurries in.*

ROSHANARA. Has the ice arrived?

ITBAR (*to* FAQIR). Excuse us, slaves fetch a daily supply from the mountains, my lady is concerned with their tardiness.

ROSHANARA. Are you being disrespectful, Itbar?

ITBAR. My lady?

ROSHANARA. Tell me as soon as it gets here.

She hurries off.

ITBAR (*to the* FAQIR). Eager to prove what a fine First Lady she would make.

FAQIR. Has the Emperor stopped his building work?

ITBAR. The Taj Mahal? A week of inactivity, but the rain is coming so they are back at it now. They have to waterproof it, which means immersing each and every brick in scalding fat.

FAQIR. That must be costly.

ITBAR. Mustn't it?

AURANGZEB (*twenty-seven*) *arrives, fresh from his travels.*

AURANGZEB. Where is my sister?

ITBAR. Prince Aurangzeb, welcome home.

AURANGZEB. Thank you, Itbar. What is this faqir doing here?

FAQIR. Salaam alaikum, Sire, I am happy to see you.

AURANGZEB. Did Father summon him?

ITBAR. He did, Sire.

AURANGZEB. Send him home.

(*To the* FAQIR.) We do not want you here.

FAQIR *doesn't know what to do.*

FAQIR. It may be polite to wait and see your father –

AURANGZEB (*interrupting*). I said leave, you worshipper of idols!

FAQIR. I am a Sufi, Sire, a Muslim, not a Hindu…

AURANGZEB. How dare you call your naked dancing, Islam?

FAQIR. Because it is, Sire. We dance for love of Allah and his Prophet, may peace be upon him, with ecstasy in our hearts.

AURANGZEB. I do not acknowledge that Islam!

DARA (*twenty-nine*) *and* SHAH JAHAN (*fifty-two*), *hurry in.* AURANGZEB *bows deeply,* FAQIR *follows suit.*

SHAH JAHAN (*to* AURANGZEB). No sooner have you crossed my threshold than you see fit to abuse my guests?

DARA. Salaam, brother, when did you arrive?

AURANGZEB. Salaam alaikum.

Bowing to SHAH JAHAN.

Your Highness.

DARA. Why don't I show you to my apartments, you can freshen up.

AURANGZEB. I'd feel safer in an apartment of my own.

SHAH JAHAN. Safer?

DARA. You have rooms of your own within mine, our section of the fort is newly built, it's secure.

AURANGZEB. I see you've ploughed funds into your building works, Father? I passed the semi-constructed mausoleum.

SHAH JAHAN. How dare you travel all this distance to pour insidious allegations on your family! Unsafe in your own brother's home?

AURANGZEB. I came to see my sister.

SHAH JAHAN. The fire was three weeks ago.

AURANGZEB. It's the first invitation in eight years that you have extended to me.

SHAH JAHAN. You have been engaged in other business.

AURANGZEB. I have, and the Deccan thrives under my leadership.

SHAH JAHAN. So do its mango trees, which you have kept close.

AURANGZEB. I have sent the fruits of every crop!

SHAH JAHAN. Do you think I don't know? You keep the best for yourself.

AURANGZEB. I would like to see my sister now.

DARA. She is sleeping…

SHAH JAHAN (*to* AURANGZEB). You will pay for this haughty and ridiculous attitude, how dare you mistrust us? Take off your sword.

AURANGZEB. Why?

SHAH JAHAN. I am stripping you of office, off!

DARA. Father…

SHAH JAHAN. You are no longer in charge of the Deccan. Ex-viceroy.

AURANGZEB *takes off his sword.*

DARA. He did not mean to offend, Father...

AURANGZEB. If ousting a conspiracy for fratricide is offensive then so be it.

SHAH JAHAN. Fratricide?

AURANGZEB *strides off.* FAQIR *follows him, while speaking to* SHAH JAHAN.

FAQIR. Your Majesty, do you mind if I speak with your son?

AURANGZEB. I do not want to see you ever again!

FAQIR. Let me talk with you, Sire...

AURANGZEB. You should have been killed a decade ago!

SHAH JAHAN. Never trust a snake in the grass.

DARA. Aurangzeb, come home with me, see the family.

FAQIR *tries to speak to* AURANGZEB.

FAQIR. It was wrong to say what I saw, I should have chosen death.

AURANGZEB. I wish you had!

DARA. Aurangzeb...

AURANGZEB. God will know our hearts!

Scene Three

We are back in 1659. JAHANARA *and* SHAH JAHAN *are led to a small room at the top of the harem tower of Agra Fort. They are more simply dressed.*

SHAH JAHAN. Dara behind bars!

ITBAR. It will be me looking after things for you now.

SHAH JAHAN *removes his jewels and hands them to* ITBAR. ITBAR *gives them to a* SERVANT, *who carries them off.*

SHAH JAHAN (*bitterly*). How comforting, to have an old friend as jailor. Spit it out, then, Itbar, don't spare the details.

ITBAR. I never saw a greater crowd, Sire, not even on your coronation. There were no flowers left in the marketplace, not a bloom, every rooftop was crammed, all thirsting for a glimpse of the broken Prince.

JAHANARA. Is Dara broken, Itbar?

ITBAR. As he passed, his petite elephant lumbering her scabbed feet through the fetid streets, they roared their outrage from those roofs and windows, every shadowy corner, 'Dara, Dara, set Dara free!' The elephant's legs shook with every step, she'd not been washed in weeks.

SHAH JAHAN. Oh, Aurangzeb!

ITBAR. You would have been warmed by the weeping, Sire, as your people saw their hopes of Prince Dara replacing you, recede. The soothsaying Faqir, who once brought you apples, danced, half-naked, intoning, 'Today is Dara's coronation, Emperor Dara is carried to his throne!'

SHAH JAHAN. If only!

ITBAR. Then the whole crowd crooned, many thousands, all different religions, 'Emperor Dara, Emperor Dara!' He inspired unity if nothing else.

JAHANARA. And Dara?

ITBAR. Like a snapped twig, ma'am, without the will to even lift his head.

JAHANARA. I knew it. I felt it.

SHAH JAHAN. How can a brother do this?

JAHANARA. Where is he now?

ITBAR. In a cell under the Red Fort.

SHAH JAHAN. He has to be freed, I cannot bear to sit here like a stuffed animal!

ITBAR. How irritating to be confined, Sire, after so many years of liberty, but your tower is pleasant, one of the peaks in what was once your fort. I know you are concerned about the cellars, with their coffers of gold and silver, but at least you can enjoy a view of your Taj Mahal.

JAHANARA. Stop it, Itbar, for old times' sake.

ITBAR. I am conceding, simply, that it is considerate of Emperor Aurangzeb to offer an outlook onto the very beautiful monument you created.

SHAH JAHAN. I can barely see the cursed thing.

ITBAR. Oh, Sire, don't call it cursed...

JAHANARA. Itbar.

SHAH JAHAN. Why is everything being obliterated, my Empire, my eyes, my son? You are all there is left, petal, and soft as dew you are, fruit of my tree.

JAHANARA. I know, Father.

SHAH JAHAN. Leave us, Itbar.

ITBAR. I'm sorry, Sire?

SHAH JAHAN. Leave us, please, can't you?

ITBAR (*taking his leave*). Of course, Sire. I may be your jailor but I can still take instruction, for old times' sake.

He goes. SHAH JAHAN *looks out of the window.*

SHAH JAHAN. It all looks mauve to me.

JAHANARA. It's dusk now, Baba, it's all I see too.

SHAH JAHAN. I intended for it to last.

JAHANARA. It is lasting.

SHAH JAHAN. Not wither and die.

He looks bitterly towards the Taj.

It proved to be merely the shadow of a woman who died too young.

JAHANARA. Some shadow, Baba, twenty thousand workers labouring seventeen years for your wife. It's a physical poem and you know it, the most exquisite monument ever.

SHAH JAHAN. A ghost, is all. Spectre-white against the red of life. Its towers are spindly arms outstretched, to Allah, to our children, to me. The arch in the middle is mine, all mine, welcoming me to her inner self, so intricate and wise. Imposing yet contained. She sprang to life when you broached her, you see, vivid curls of green tendrils and blood-red flowers. She stood sentry to our lives, look at those lives now. I see nothing of it, Jahanara, just a mid-distance smear.

JAHANARA. You see me, don't you?

SHAH JAHAN. Stand by the light, let me look.

She poses for him, slightly reluctant.

I miss her so much.

JAHANARA. I know.

SHAH JAHAN. I held my softness for her.

JAHANARA. Yes, Baba. And some for me.

Scene Four

*The throne room of the Red Fort, Delhi. There is a sense of
urgency.* AURANGZEB *paces, his* COURTIERS *await
instruction.* HIRA BAI, *in another world, is washing, and
humming. She tries to remember the Wudu – hands, three times,
mouth, spit, three times.* ROSHANARA, *half-veiled, is with the*
COURTIERS. AURANGZEB *indicates for her to leave.*

AURANGZEB. Roshanara.

ROSHANARA. I thought I might add my voice to the debate?

AURANGZEB. You think it's your place?

ROSHANARA *shrugs.*

When I want you, I will invite you. Go.

ROSHANARA. I will be all ears.

AURANGZEB *dismisses her. She goes behind the screen.*
HIRA BAI *also leaves.*

AURANGZEB. Gentlemen?

DANISHMAND. If I may, Your Highness, yes, the crowd is
excitable – they know he's in your dungeons – but once he's
moved off the premises, Prince Dara will become history.

AURANGZEB. Khan?

SHAISTA KHAN. Sire, that crowd is peopled with Hindus,
Christians, Jews, Yogis, Atheists… these are Dara's
supporters, not men with power in this city – where are the
aristocrats, where are the mullahs? I didn't see them out
there throwing flowers.

MULLAH FAROOQ *mutters.*

MULLAH FAROOQ. I should hope not.

SHAISTA KHAN. It is the homeless, the students, the artists, of
course they are overexcited, it is their nature to be so.

AURANGZEB. The streets are full.

SHAISTA KHAN. I don't deny the rabble is large, Sire, nor do I propose that all good Muslims are indoors. They are curious too. What I am saying is that, as Danishmand suggests, it is a transient outburst, certainly not a threat to your reign.

AURANGZEB. And your view on him staying in our dungeons?

SHAISTA KHAN. It signifies a clear throne. You can begin proceedings for an elaborate and highly visible coronation. I think it is crucial to trumpet a confident start to your reign, Sire, having acceded so hastily and quietly all those weeks ago.

ROSHANARA *appears*.

AURANGZEB. Roshanara, what is it?

ROSHANARA. I wanted to tell you, Sire, that Malik Jiwan has been attacked by the crowd.

SHAISTA KHAN. Malik Jiwan?

AURANGZEB. They hate him for handing Dara over. What happened?

ROSHANARA. He was riding down Chandni Chowk. Apparently, at first there were just a few jeers, then a woman threw muck at him, then, before he could even respond, everybody joined in with stones, pots and, from the high-up windows, the contents of their latrines.

AURANGZEB. And?

ROSHANARA. Our soldiers beat back the crowd, then brought him to the royal guest house.

AURANGZEB. He's here now?

ROSHANARA. Yes.

AURANGZEB. Release him.

ROSHANARA *smiles in understanding*.

Give him something for leading me to Dara then let him loose, without guards, without soldiers.

DANISHMAND. Unprotected, Your Majesty, the crowd will kill him...

AURANGZEB. Do you propose I intervene with Allah, Danishmand? They want meat so give them meat, it might assuage their hysterics.

ROSHANARA *leaves*.

The man betrayed his benefactor, it would not be long before he deceived us too. Now, to the matter in hand, my brother in our dungeons. Anyone?

AURANGZEB *ascends to the Peacock Throne, sitting metres above his men*.

DANISHMAND. Your Majesty, Prince Dara has met his fate.

AURANGZEB. Your point, Danishmand?

DANISHMAND. His whole life he expected to succeed your father, even before Shah Jahan made him Crown Prince it was clear that Dara would accede.

AURANGZEB. Go on.

DANISHMAND. He felt it was his, the Empire. And then, despite all your father's extra soldiers, you defeated him.

AURANGZEB. God was on our side.

DANISHMAND. But from his position, he had the base materials, he was brave...

SHAISTA KHAN. He wasn't practised. (*To* AURANGZEB.) You, Sire, went on campaign after campaign, Dara stayed home and read.

(*To* DANISHMAND.) Like you.

DANISHMAND. A philosopher, yes.

AURANGZEB *is losing patience with* DANISHMAND.

AURANGZEB. Your notions are fascinating, Danishmand, but progress your point.

DANISHMAND. Apologies, Sire, I know I can be circuitous.
What I'm saying is, for Dara to have lost is enough, ample
humiliation. Therefore, I propose Gwalior prison, let him sit
and read in the dark for the rest of his days.

AURANGZEB. And what do you say to the fact that my father
spared none of his brothers at succession?

DANISHMAND. Was it necessary? All his predecessors, no
less vehement in pursuit of the throne, stopped short of
killing. Your religion, Sire, your mercy, and your bloodline,
call for sparing your brother's life.

MIR KHALIL. Your Holy Majesty, may I speak?

AURANGZEB. Speak, Khalil.

MIR KHALIL. You struggled hard for rights within this family,
and look at it now. Sixty days on a camel's back to cross
your Empire, Sire, from the Deccan to Kashmir, from Bengal
to the Punjab, everything is yours. Your father wasted
resources on opulent monuments but you, Sire, will expand
and consolidate this Empire.

AURANGZEB. Don't flatter me, cousin.

MIR KHALIL. I wouldn't, cousin.

   AURANGZEB *addresses all his councillors.*

AURANGZEB. Don't be so salty that I have to spit you out, nor
so cloying that I choke on you.

MIR KHALIL. All I'm meaning is that nothing should hold you
back. So long as Prince Dara lives, in or out of prison, he
could incite mutiny. Sire, I think that killing him would be
conducive to the common good.

   Taking their cue from AURANGZEB*'s interest, the others
   are attentive to* MIR KHALIL*'s speech.*

AURANGZEB. Shaista Khan?

SHAISTA KHAN. Perhaps. Prince Dara will be a hanging
sword while he lives. Murad is no threat, he can waste in

prison for as long as it takes, but Dara...? Dara inspires love, and love, as we know, is dangerous.

AURANGZEB *doesn't like this.*

They are beguiled, of course, his followers, but they are numerous. Were he in a cell next to Murad, whenever there was a law the dissenters didn't like they'd riot outside the prison, so I do agree with everything Mir Khalil says, with one exception. We cannot just kill Dara. If he had died in the war, all well and good, but he did not. The crowds have seen and screamed for him.

AURANGZEB. He is a threat to my rule.

SHAISTA KHAN. Beheading a popular rebel makes us feel safe, temporarily. If you'd killed him in battle the question, 'How would it be were Dara Emperor?' would not prevail, but execute him as a political prisoner and that question will fill people's minds for the length of your lifetime. It could even inspire rebellion in the unconquered regions.

AURANGZEB. How do we quell such doubts?

SHAISTA KHAN. If you would allow Mullah Farooq to speak, I think there may yet be a third way.

AURANGZEB (*to* MULLAH FAROOQ). Your thoughts, revered Mawlana.

MULLAH FAROOQ. Your Majesty, you are the highest embodiment of knowledge on religion and warfare...

AURANGZEB. Not over-salty nor too sugary...

MULLAH FAROOQ. You have defeated Dara – politically he is isolated, the governors and gentry are with you, physically he is imprisoned – yet there is a piece of ground where he remains undefeated.

AURANGZEB. Which ground?

MULLAH FAROOQ. The high ground, he is morally strong. He has spent time developing his mind, and his search for the commonality between people can make him seem, saintly.

AURANGZEB. Saintly? His eclectic, laissez-faire attitude sickens me, I'm surprised he didn't call his sons Deepak and Richard.

MULLAH FAROOQ. Unfortunately, however, people adore him. Even a small faction of the aristocracy! As Governor Khan iterated, were Dara to be assassinated as a political rebel, he would certainly die a luminary and that, you cannot afford, Sire.

AURANGZEB. Agreed.

MULLAH FAROOQ. Therefore it is not just his physical form that must perish, but also his mythology.

Beat.

AURANGZEB. How?

MULLAH FAROOQ. Were it proven that Dara defied, not only a brother, but flouted God himself, an Islamic ruler would be invoked to take serious action.

AURANGZEB. Though the Quran advises us not to sever ourselves from our family?

MULLAH FAROOQ. The greater divine injunction would speak to Dara's desertion of Islam, were it proved that he no longer upheld Islam's supremacy and could therefore be called – an infidel.

Beat.

AURANGZEB. Mullah, how much evidence is there for such an accusation?

MULLAH FAROOQ. I have been gathering particulars, your honour. My administrators have prepared a file on Dara's religious eccentricities.

AURANGZEB. I appreciate your careful attention, Mullah Farooq.

(*To* MIR KHALIL.) Make a public announcement, Prince Dara will be tried for apostasy.

His AIDES *are surprised at the suddenness of this decision.*

I have been exalted to this position because our Lord, who raises the meek and abases the haughty, determined it should be so.

(*To* MULAH FAROOQ.) When this is over, I would like to compile an exhaustive compendium of Islamic law, every permutation of life from the Islamic perspective. This will be a bedrock for generations, we must be thorough, we will consolidate and augment the path, our instructions are clear. The name says it all, 'the course to be followed', the 'Sharia' path. And remember, all of you, at all times, that God made me Emperor because I defend his word. Gentlemen, you are dismissed.

The COURTIERS *leave.* ROSHANARA *reappears.*

ROSHANARA. You'll try him in court? How clever.

AURANGZEB. Clever?

ROSHANARA. Shrewd to have found yourself a devious mullah.

AURANGZEB. Do not judge him, Roshanara, Allah himself is the most creative of thinkers.

ROSHANARA. You and Allah both, brother. I knew you'd be an inspiring ruler.

AURANGZEB. My inspiration is Islam, sister, nothing more and nothing less than its ultimate nobility.

ACT THREE

Scene One

Agra Fort. AFIA *approaches* ITBAR *with a tray.*

AFIA. I hear Dara is going to court?

ITBAR. There is no limit to what families do to one another, so much crueller than they are to strangers.

AFIA. What does the Emperor think?

ITBAR. Who, Aurangzeb?

AFIA. Shah Jahan.

ITBAR. He's not Emperor any more, you can stop calling him that.

AFIA. It's a difficult habit to break. Does this smell odd to you?

ITBAR *sniffs the food.*

This plate, the other is for Jahanara.

ITBAR. It smells fine.

AFIA. Maybe I'm being suspicious. We don't need this separate cook, the kitchens can manage perfectly well, but the instruction came that the Emperor –

ITBAR. Who?

AFIA. Aurangzeb's *baba* needed separate food because of his age and infirmity.

ITBAR *laughs.* AFIA *is about the only person who makes him laugh.*

ITBAR. As if diet could cure failing eyesight and an insatiable desire for coitus.

AFIA. Not something you suffer from, the eyes nor the other.

Silence. This hurts him.

ITBAR. I am not fully a man, Afia, you know that.

AFIA. Some girls wouldn't care – they'd be happy just to be held.

ITBAR. Nor are my eyes blighted, as you accurately pointed out. You are a very beautiful girl, Afia...

AFIA *steps towards him, he backs away.*

I cannot!

She backs off.

AFIA. When Mumtaz Mahal was alive, Shah Jahan was more moderate, wasn't he?

ITBAR. Though she did have fourteen pregnancies.

AFIA. Poor Queen.

ITBAR. How are your two, without their father?

AFIA *weighs* ITBAR *up.*

AFIA. I don't see them enough, but my mother manages.

ITBAR. If there's anything I can do...

AFIA. No. I shouldn't worry about the food?

ITBAR. If Aurangzeb was poisoning his father, Afia, I wouldn't care.

AFIA. That's not true, Itbar, you talk such nonsense.

ITBAR. No, I don't.

AFIA. You bathe his eyes each morning!

ITBAR. So? Shah Jahan has earned his son's hatred, but, Jahanara samples everything. Go back to the kitchens, try it on one of the dogs.

AFIA. They're expecting their lunch...

ITBAR. They are prisoners, they must abide by our schedules now.

AFIA. I can't help pitying them.

ITBAR. Because your heart is soft, Afia. May it always remain so.

Scene Two

Red Fort, Delhi. ROSHANARA is smoking a hookah.

ROSHANARA. Will you see Dara before tomorrow?

AURANGZEB. I'm not a fan of your new habit, sister.

ROSHANARA. It relaxes me. You don't like the smell?

AURANGZEB. It's too sweet, like apples.

ROSHANARA. I observe God's rules, but I also understand earthly laws.

AURANGZEB. Such as?

ROSHANARA. *Ya takht ya tabut*, throne or tomb. If Dara lives, Aurangzeb, I will fear for my life, and so should you. It scares me.

AURANGZEB. If he lives, he will be in prison.

ROSHANARA. But he knows whose side I am on.

AURANGZEB. It could do more to relax you, that hookah.

IMAD *appears.*

Yes?

IMAD. Your sister is here, Sire.

ROSHANARA *leaps up.*

ROSHANARA. And he doesn't mean me!

AURANGZEB. Make her wait, Imad. Is the astrologer ready?

IMAD. Yes, my lord.

AURANGZEB. Send him in.

IMAD *leaves*.

ROSHANARA. What does she want?

AURANGZEB. What do you think?

ROSHANARA. Anything for Dara.

AURANGZEB. She is a good sister.

ROSHANARA. Would she do the same for you?

IMAD *shows the* ASTROLOGER *in. He bows deeply to* AURANGZEB.

(*To the* ASTROLOGER.) Tell us what the stars say for tomorrow, it better be good.

AURANGZEB. Wait. On second thoughts, we'll hear from you later. (*To* IMAD.) Show Jahanara in.

The ASTROLOGER *is wrong-footed but bows and retreats as* IMAD *shows him out*.

ROSHANARA. Why do you honour her so much, she has backed Dara for ever!

AURANGZEB. She is kind-hearted and wise, Roshanara, which cannot always be said of you.

IMAD *returns with* JAHANARA.

JAHANARA. Salaam, brother, sister, greetings, Your Majesty.

She kisses AURANGZEB*'s hand*.

AURANGZEB. How are things at Agra?

JAHANARA. Father is losing his sight, and hopes of a visit from his Emperor son.

AURANGZEB. There is much to attend to here.

JAHANARA. Like trying your brother for apostasy?

ROSHANARA. See, she will try and persuade you out of it!

JAHANARA. Of course I will! You are putting on trial one of the most devoted men ever.

ROSHANARA. How do you know, you've only encountered Sufis and eunuchs?

JAHANARA. It is a perversion of Islam to put Dara on trial.

AURANGZEB. Careful, Jahanara, I may be your brother but I am also the keeper of our faith, it is my destiny.

JAHANARA. Is it Dara's destiny to be tried for attempting to understand his people?

AURANGZEB. They are not his people, they are my people, and before that they were Father's.

JAHANARA. Dara is a sage, Aurangzeb.

AURANGZEB. Then why did he come to the battlefield?

JAHANARA. Because Father urged him and our disparate Empire needs him!

ROSHANARA. Well, it can't have him!

AURANGZEB. Let me do the talking.

ROSHANARA. Remind her what a thief Dara is, how he stole Baba's love and never shared it!

JAHANARA. Those were Father's mistakes, not Dara's. He was a boy, Roshanara, spoiled, as we all were.

AURANGZEB. We reap as we sow.

JAHANARA. But we are adults now, or at least we are meant to be!

ROSHANARA (*in* AURANGZEB*'s ear*). Tell her to go!

Beat.

JAHANARA. I'm glad to have the opportunity to congratulate you, brother. I am proud of you.

AURANGZEB. Thank you.

JAHANARA. Show mercy, Aurangzeb, don't go through with the trial. You have the throne, Dara cannot take it from you.

ROSHANARA. Stop it, Jahanara.

JAHANARA. You both adored Dara when you were younger.

ROSHANARA. Before we knew better.

JAHANARA. Who knows better than an instinctive child, Roshanara?

(*Quietly, to* AURANGZEB.) Allah is merciful and compassionate.

AURANGZEB. He is also just and the avenger.

JAHANARA. Put down your cudgel, Aurangzeb.

AURANGZEB. I am not a vengeful man.

JAHANARA. I know you're not! If he is found guilty, Aurangzeb... You would not want to be responsible for extinguishing that bright human light, would you?

AURANGZEB. The bright light of Dara, he has so much for nothing.

JAHANARA. Can you hold that against a man? He is a generous soul.

AURANGZEB. For their wedding I gave Dara and Nadira a set of fine bone European china I excelled myself to find, as well as jewels costing nearly half a year's salary – he never thanked me. Because I have never been more than useless to him.

JAHANARA. He was a busy newly-wed, Aurangzeb, he would hate to know he had forgotten to thank you. It is difficult for the older one always to remember –

AURANGZEB (*interrupting*). The slave girls laughed in my face for a year and he never stopped them!

JAHANARA. Which girls?

AURANGZEB. At Grandfather's, but I forgive all that.

ROSHANARA. You shouldn't.

AURANGZEB. I forgive him, Jahanara.

Beat.

ROSHANARA. Excuse me, but what do you mean, brother?

AURANGZEB. We only take good deeds and character to our graves, I here declare to you both that I pardon Dara.

JAHANARA. This is such exquisite news...

ROSHANARA. What are you saying, brother?

JAHANARA. He will cause you no trouble, he will do nothing but read and pray for you...

ROSHANARA. You cannot do this, Aurangzeb, we will never have real power if Dara lives!

JAHANARA. I am flooded with gratitude, my soul feels twinned with Dara's.

AURANGZEB. In myself I absolve him –

ROSHANARA. Aurangzeb!

AURANGZEB. But I cannot let my personal feelings override Sharia law. He will go to trial.

JAHANARA. No, Aurangzeb...

AURANGZEB. If the judge discovers Dara to be an enemy of Islam, I am powerless against that ruling.

ROSHANARA. That's my Emperor.

JAHANARA. We have been through so much, survived this long...

AURANGZEB (*to* JAHANARA). I am sorry, sister, but when it comes to choosing between family or faith, my judge's verdict is final.

JAHANARA. Please, Aurangzeb!

AURANGZEB. Put the sun and the moon in the palms of my hands, I will not bend from duty.

ROSHANARA. What if the judge finds him innocent?

AURANGZEB. As I said, it is beyond my control.

Scene Three

Courtroom, Delhi, 1659. The room is full of men. Up behind the marble screen are the shadows of women. DARA *is brought in, hands and feet fettered.*

QAZI SAYED. Court commences. Counsel bringing the case against the accused, stand.

PROSECUTOR TALIB *stands.*

Counsel defending the accused, stand.

DARA *stands.*

You are defending yourself, Prince, he's defending himself?

DARA. I am, your honour.

QAZI SAYED. We can't have him like this. Remove the leg restraints, but keep the hand fetters on.

GUARDS *release* DARA *from his place.*

Stand the Prince there. Today, the twenty-ninth day of August, 1659, Prince Dara Shikoh is here to be tried for the crime of apostasy, punishable by death. We will test the accused's acceptance or disavowal of the superiority and definitiveness of Islam. Ready to proceed?

PROSECUTOR TALIB. Affirmative, your honour.

DARA (*at the same time as* PROSECUTOR TALIB). Yes, your honour.

QAZI SAYED. I call the Counsel for the Prosecution.

PROSECUTOR TALIB *steps up*.

Your first witness?

PROSECUTOR TALIB. My one and only witness, the accused.

QAZI SAYED (*to* DARA). A busy day for you, Prince. Onto the witness stand. Do you swear by Allah to tell the truth and only the truth in this court?

DARA. By Allah I do.

QAZI SAYED. Prosecutor, proceed.

PROSECUTOR TALIB. Thank you.

When a man wilfully strays from Islam, it is the most profound defection. When this man is a prince, for so many years the Crown Prince, admired by every child in the Empire, such deviation is unpardonable. Left to his own devices, this particular man could mislead every subject in this land. My prediction for today is that we will expose that the accused standing here is every last inch the living embodiment of this perilous desertion.

QAZI SAYED. Proceed.

PROSECUTOR TALIB. Without further ado, let us open with the first blazing fact against the accused. You went to some lengths, did you not, Prince Dara, engaging the help of Hindu pundits, to translate certain Sanskrit texts in to Persian? Texts which you have blithely called, 'God's most perfect revelation'. I refer, of course, to the ancient Hindu writings, the Upanishads, can you confirm you had these works translated?

DARA. I can.

PROSECUTOR TALIB. Stories passed down, from Hindu to Hindu.

DARA. The most wise offerings, yes.

PROSECUTOR TALIB. What exactly is it that they reveal?

DARA. You've not read them, Prosecutor?

PROSECUTOR TALIB. No, I am a Muslim.

DARA. I did not know that being a Muslim meant being ignorant of other cultures.

PROSECUTOR TALIB. Tell us, since you're such an avid reader of them, about the Upanishads, Prince.

DARA. They are philosophical discussions about God's universe. They speak of our physical, astrological and spiritual worlds being linked. They predate the Quran and I am convinced that they are one of the blessed books referred to in the Quran.

PROSECUTOR TALIB. Convinced are you?

DARA. The hidden source the Quran acknowledges as being the fountainhead of monotheism.

PROSECUTOR TALIB. Monotheism predating Islam?

DARA. And all the Abrahamic faiths.

PROSECUTOR TALIB. Making Islam simply another in a long line of religions, Prince Dara?

DARA. Not simply that to me, Prosecutor, seeing as it is my religion.

PROSECUTOR TALIB. You shall not be the judge of that today.

There's an appreciative murmur from the benches.

As we will illustrate, your interests flail around so wildly, Prince, you seem unable to stick even to monotheistic religions. One God, several hundred, you're not particular. Tell us, while we're on the matter, is it or is it not true that you are a self-proclaimed friend of this new cult religion, the Sikhs?

DARA. I am sympathetic to their beliefs, if that casts me as a friend, then yes.

PROSECUTOR TALIB. Their beliefs being something of a hybrid – a bit of Hinduism, a pinch of Islam...

DARA. The best of both.

PROSECUTOR TALIB. Oh, so we can pick and choose from God's words, can we, improve on his universe?

DARA. The Quran has everything, is my everything, but I do also appreciate the value in the Hindu texts. The Sikhs, young though they are, look to both these magnificent religions for guidance and inspiration – accept His will, be humble, be courageous...

PROSECUTOR TALIB. Dara Shikoh, tell us, are you a secret Sikh?

DARA. No, I am a Muslim who recognises that other religions have value.

PROSECUTOR TALIB. Equal value to Islam?

DARA. I cannot say equal, yet ultimately they lead to the same understanding, or very similar.

There is a ripple through the court.

PROSECUTOR TALIB. As anticipated, my witness is providing all the evidence against himself that we could possibly wish for.

DARA. What kind of evidence, Prosecutor – a sign of religious knowledge? That can only count against me when looked at from a deficit of reading and imagination.

PROSECUTOR TALIB (*sharp*). I advise you, Prince, to hold your tongue before you insult me further. What you say here in court and have said every day of your life since you were teenaged, is blasphemous and a deviation from the path of Islam.

DARA. It is not, and furthermore, you and your cronies have been stacking ammunition against me, twisting each word I utter, every day of my life since I was teenaged, Prosecutor Talib.

QAZI SAYED *speaks to* DARA.

QAZI SAYED. You can explain yourself further when you are running your defence, right now it is the Prosecutor's line of questioning.

PROSECUTOR TALIB. Thank you, Qazi. Let us speed on, past countless other heretical translations, the Bhagavad Gita itself, for example, to which we can return if the need presents itself, and attend to the accused's own written works. *The Mingling of Two Oceans* – this book was authored by you?

DARA. It was.

PROSECUTOR TALIB. 'Mingling'?

DARA. The commonality between Islam and Hinduism.

PROSECUTOR TALIB. Islam and Hinduism being the two 'oceans'?

DARA. If you like.

PROSECUTOR TALIB. I don't like. Am I the only one here for whom that idea seems strikingly similar to the aforementioned Sikhs, to mingle or should we say, mangle, different religions? To imagine that Islam takes its place alongside Hinduism or any other 'sea'.

DARA. That is fact, Prosecutor, ours is one of many different systems of faith in the world.

PROSECUTOR TALIB. So, you believe, frankly, Prince, that the Hindu faith is as valid as the Muslim faith?

DARA. To a Hindu, it is.

PROSECUTOR TALIB. Therefore Islam is not supreme?

There is a commotion as SIPIHR *is brought in to the courtroom in chains.*

DARA. Sipihr!

DARA *is deeply distressed to see his son.*

SIPIHR. I wasn't able to run any more, Father, I'm sorry.

DARA. Have they hurt you, did you hurt him?

He addresses this last question to the marble screens where the women are. The court, murmuring, turn to look at where he is looking.

QAZI SAYED. Silence in court, sit the boy down.

DARA. I have not seen my son, Qazi, since being captured...

SIPIHR *is forced to sit down.*

QAZI SAYED. Now is not the time for a reunion, Prince Dara. Prosecutor Talib, please continue your questioning.

PROSECUTOR TALIB. Prince Dara, let me ask you once more, now that the latecomers have settled, is Islam supreme?

DARA, *utterly electrified by* SIPIHR*'s arrival, lets down his guard.*

DARA. Who cares which door you open to come into the light?

SIPIHR *tries to stand but is forced back down.*
PROSECUTOR TALIB *strings out his advantage.*

PROSECUTOR TALIB. The Qazi here cares, your son, Prince Sipihr appears to care, and I would be most surprised if our honourable Emperor did not care. '*La 'ilaha 'illallah muhammadur rasulullah.* There is no God but Allah and Muhammad is his messenger', yet, for you, any old door will do?

DARA *opens his mouth to speak but* PROSECUTOR TALIB *stops him.*

In your book, which I *have* read, you posit that Hinduism and Islam share so many characteristics that they could almost be yoked. Tell us, Prince Dara, as we would dearly love to know, how can Islam, our monotheistic single-pointed religion, *mingle* with a religion which worships cattle and has endless numbers of gods? 'There is no God but Allah and Muhammad is his messenger.'

DARA. Look beneath. Beyond the glaring separation, you will discover the same desire to know God, the same attempt to live better lives, to help us reach meaning. Examine the impulse behind their systems, Prosecutor, the religions share utterly an understanding of what it is to be human.

PROSECUTOR TALIB. A human Muslim, a human Hindu or a human Sikh?

DARA. Prosecutor Talib, explain to us, what is the difference?

SIPIHR *is squirming, hearing his father speak. From behind the screen there is a haughty laugh, it sounds distinctly like* ROSHANARA*'s*.

PROSECUTOR TALIB. So you could just as easily call yourself a Hindu or a Sikh?

DARA. Of course I couldn't because I am Muslim, but my humanness is shared with anyone and everyone. If we choose to love one special person, does it mean that they are the only person worthy of loving? 'To you, your religion, to me, mine.' 'There is no obligation in religion' – straight from the Quran. We cannot force our religion upon others.

PROSECUTOR TALIB. Can't we?

DARA. We reach for God because we want to, because he shapes our lives, there should be no coercion in worship.

PROSECUTOR TALIB. Oh, so we should do what we like, pray when we want and not when we don't want?

DARA. Who said discipline is not useful? I only say that our duty as Muslims, whose God tells us there is no obligation in religion, is to allow all faiths to flourish. Is that not what our Empire is built on, the very reason the Mughals are great? We were the minority, who were we to march in to new territory and impose our creed on a massive majority of different faiths? Babur knew that, Akbar the Great knew it, Jahangir knew it. They each had weaknesses but they all embraced the range of beliefs within their Empire. Babur, founder of it all, banned cow slaughter in Delhi out of respect. Shah Jahan's own mother was Hindu! Open-mindedness is the wellspring of who we are, and what an Empire! Our monuments, our paintings, books to die for –

PROSECUTOR TALIB (*speaking over him, ironically*). Prophetically spoken...

DARA (*ignoring him*). – our music! These expressions of our humanity have poured forth from variety. Akbar's genius was to harness different traditions and his reward was a vibrant, prosperous kingdom. Akbar made his governors read poems by Rumi!

PROSECUTOR TALIB. Sorry to interrupt your diatribe, Prince, but let me ask you directly – are you a polytheist, do you, like the Hindus, worship many gods?

DARA. One God, your God.

PROSECUTOR TALIB. Mine is not easily mistaken for a Hindu or a Christian God.

DARA. Allah is God of all, not just the Muhammadans. 'It is revealed to me by inspiration that your Allah is one Allah', who spoke this, Prosecutor?

PROSECUTOR TALIB. I am the examiner.

QAZI SAYED. Answer the accused's question if you don't mind.

The QAZI is becoming absorbed by DARA's argument.

PROSECUTOR TALIB. Muhammad, may peace be upon him, who also said that two religions cannot coexist in the Arabian Peninsula!

DARA. But that is a survival argument, not a spiritual one.

PROSECUTOR TALIB. Are you calling Muhammad, peace be upon him, a strategist?

DARA. Of course, partly. Muhammad, peace be upon him, said those things in a single moment. As he admitted himself, he was but a man.

PROSECUTOR TALIB. Now you reduce him to mortal status and call him fickle? Is that how you feel about the Quran, Prince Dara, do you consider it, secretly, made of dispensable ideas?

DARA. I am worn down and my heart is full, please forgive my inadequacies in expressing myself. I struggle with describing my faith to others.

PROSECUTOR TALIB. Never mind that you've written hundreds of poems on the matter!

DARA. I cannot undo knowing Allah as I do. He exists in every cell of my being, He is my entirety, I am a drop and He is the sea.

PROSECUTOR TALIB. But which sea, Prince Dara?

DARA *chooses to ignore* PROSECUTOR TALIB*'s provocation.*

DARA. It is undermining to Allah to imagine he refuses people because of the path they walk to him on.

PROSECUTOR TALIB. 'If anyone desires a religion other than Islam, never will it be accepted of Him and in the hereafter he will be in the ranks of the losers.'

DARA. Muhammad, may peace be upon him, had to be extreme in that moment, he was building his religion.

PROSECUTOR TALIB. This is the holy Quran we are talking about, God's word, what are you saying, Prince? Careful now, are you proposing that the Quran is not the word of God?

There is extreme tension from the benches, and from behind the women's screen.

DARA. I propose no such thing.

PROSECUTOR TALIB. You implied that it was subject to the will of man, to Muhammad's, may peace be upon him, fluctuations, inferring that the Quran itself has mutability.

DARA. Of course the Quran is the word of God, because it comes from that place which is the heart of the world. But as a document, it is also bound up with the specifics of the time and place from whence it sprang.

SIPIHR. Father...

Another amazed laugh from ROSHANARA, *more consternation in the benches.*

DARA. The Arab desert is not a Mughal city.

PROSECUTOR TALIB. Do go on.

DARA. The Quran is a text that will last us for ever, serving us all to life's end, but Allah works in mysterious ways. He is lively in his endeavours to touch us, he shifts his form, he reaches through time, across latitudes, reshaping his teaching, sculpting it according to our needs. If we do not accept other faiths, we destroy the foundation of religion itself! They are the different pigments used by our Divine painter, which means that whomsoever we are, if we are still enough or curious enough, we come to know Allah.

PROSECUTOR TALIB. You call it stillness to sample the gamut of religions like a bee in spring?

DARA. Prosecutor, at the centre of every blossom is honey, the rest, frankly, is ritual.

PROSECUTOR TALIB. Sign your own death sentence, Prince Dara.

DARA. It was signed before I stepped in here, Prosecutor.

A beat. SIPIHR'*s heart is in his mouth, everything is very quiet.* PROSECUTOR TALIB *rallies and proceeds.*

PROSECUTOR TALIB. Moving on from your take-it-or-leave-it relationship with the Quran –

DARA (*interrupting*). That is entirely unfair –

PROSECUTOR TALIB (*interrupting*). 'Paradise is where there is no mullah.' Recognise your words?

DARA. Do you not agree, Prosecutor? In paradise, surely you would hope not to be told how to live by others?

PROSECUTOR TALIB. Will you admit in court that you have no respect for the religious men of Islam?

DARA. Point to me which one and I shall tell you.

PROSECUTOR TALIB. Don't get clever with me, Prince. You agree with Nanak, the Sikh teacher, who said, 'The Qazis' – (*To* QAZI SAYED.) forgive me, your honour, this is not my sentiment, 'who sit in court and minister justice, commit injustice if their palms are not greased'?

DARA. Men are corruptible, why should religious scholars be different? Guru Nanak was merely commenting on the ones who do not practise what they preach.

PROSECUTOR TALIB. You very comfortably call that man a Guru when the Muslim faith does not concede to such a notion!

DARA. It is difficult to grasp this world, don't you agree, Prosecutor? Even after Muhammad, God's final messenger, peace be upon him, I do believe God continued to send help, and that Guru Nanak was one such blessed helper.

PROSECUTOR TALIB. May I remind your honour that Nanak was a Sikh.

QAZI SAYED. I know who Nanak was, I am not asleep up here.

PROSECUTOR TALIB. Do you dispense with the five daily prayers, Prince Dara?

DARA. I'd never be so foolish.

PROSECUTOR TALIB. Do you skip Ramadan?

DARA. Prayer and fasting are water and air to me, along with charity – three of Allah's pillars. But what lies beneath these structures is the crucial thing.

PROSECUTOR TALIB. Thank you so much for correcting my misconception.

The QAZI *raises an eyebrow at* PROSECUTOR TALIB*'s sarcasm.*

If the pillars are surplus to requirement, why did the Prophet, may peace be upon him, pray?

DARA. I don't mean to trivialise our desire to reach God. We grapple our passions through prayer – hopelessness, fear, hatred – feelings we all have – praying turns the tide, allows us scope to appreciate others, but it is not more important than life itself. Muhammad, may peace be upon him, was the first to say, go out, give service, piety of the heart trumps prayer. And if we are sick or cooking, man or woman, we should not haul ourselves from our beds or kitchens to pray.

PROSECUTOR TALIB. Yet He never missed a prayer.

DARA. How do you know? When a woman came to him to say her husband had become so pious he spent all night at the mosque, what did Muhammad, may peace be upon him, do? He sent the man home, telling him to spend time with his wife and family. Maybe once, twice, the Prophet, may peace be upon him, was exhausted or calming a crying child, and, without it being recorded, omitted to pray.

ROSHANARA (*from behind the screen*). Blasphemy!

QAZI SAYED. Order!

PROSECUTOR TALIB. It's unorthodox to include female heckling but, in this instance, I must concur.

DARA. Your thinking is so narrow.

PROSECUTOR TALIB. I beg your pardon?

DARA. Forgive me.

PROSECUTOR TALIB. Go on, tell us what you really think.

DARA. You take these religious tenets as if they were sticks to beat us with, yet our Prophet, peace be upon him, could not be but responsive to the circumstances which encircled him. Yet we have seized on every one of his words, as relayed by other mutable men, as immovable truths, frozen. We know from our own lives that as soon as we seize on something as fact, it ossifies, then becomes alien. Because time changes everything. Babies become adults, water becomes desert, hatred softens. Nanak is a valuable guide because he thinks for himself whereas the mullahs, not all, I don't mean all... follow the word of God as relayed by his Prophet, peace be upon him, then recorded and passed down in the Sunnas and the Hadiths, with their different opinions and interpretations, as if it were law.

PROSECUTOR TALIB. It is law.

DARA. It was not offered up as such.

PROSECUTOR TALIB. I'll ask you for the second time, Prince, do you deny that the Quran is God's word?

DARA. I don't, Prosecutor, it is the ultimate gift from God, but the mullahs use its words like weapons, to chastise, berate and murder, which is not what they were intended for.

PROSECUTOR TALIB. Tell us, oh wise one, what you think they were intended for?

QAZI SAYED. Refrain from sarcasm in my court, Prosecutor.

PROSECUTOR TALIB. Forgive me, your honour.

DARA. You're a Muslim, you tell us why we were given the Quran?

PROSECUTOR TALIB. Am I on trial here, is my relationship found wanting with my religion?

DARA. Unfortunately not, Prosecutor.

QAZI SAYED. Order in court, it is not appropriate for the witness to speak to the Prosecutor in this way.

DARA. I am also Counsel for the Defence, your honour...

QAZI SAYED. Yes, but not yet, not in the same moment. Return to your questions, Prosecutor.

PROSECUTOR TALIB. What is the purpose of Islam?

DARA. To realise the best in ourselves.

PROSECUTOR TALIB. Yet that best can be found in any old dargah or temple, and Nanak is better than a mullah?

DARA. If we judge others by whether they bury or burn their dead, then religion has not worked.

PROSECUTOR TALIB *goes in for the kill.*

PROSECUTOR TALIB. I put to the court that the accused, Prince Dara, flagrantly betrays the very first pillar of Islam – there is no God but God and Muhammad is his messenger!

DARA. In which way do I betray it? I know this with all my being, it is my search, my sole purpose. There is one God, all paths lead to him and the Prophet Muhammad, may peace be upon him, was his greatest messenger.

PROSECUTOR TALIB. You see how he added 'greatest', your honour, did you hear?

QAZI SAYED. I did.

DARA. How can you argue with it? We are not told that He is God's *only* messenger, there were one hundred and twenty-four thousand messengers before Muhammad, may peace be upon him. What about Jesus, and Abraham…?

PROSECUTOR TALIB. Show the court your hands.

DARA. My hands?

PROSECUTOR TALIB. I would like to share with the court the writing on the inside of Prince Dara's ring. Take the jewellery off, pass it to the Qazi.

DARA *removes his ring, a* COURT ATTENDANT *delivers it to* QAZI SAYED.

Tell us about the inscription on the inside.

DARA. It says God.

PROSECUTOR TALIB. Does it, G–O–D?

DARA. In Arabic and Sanskrit.

PROSECUTOR TALIB. The Sanskrit word being?

DARA. Prabhu.

PROSECUTOR TALIB. Your honour, the accused wears this ring, not a gift but something he had commissioned himself, with the cover-all Hindu word for 'master' inscribed on it.

DARA. Also, 'Allah'.

PROSECUTOR TALIB. How magnanimous of you. Do you also have 'Allah' carved into your cross, Prince Dara, the Christian cross you wear, at all times, around your neck?

DARA *doesn't say anything. He knows the* PROSECUTOR *is closing in.*

Prince Dara, it is unpalatably clear from these proceedings, exactly as I predicted, that you strayed, long, long ago, from the pure path of Islam. Fact after fact, piece of evidence after piece of evidence. I hereby propose, Dara Shikoh, that this court finds you, unequivocally, an apostate of Islam.

QAZI SAYED. Leave the pronouncements to me, will you, Prosecutor?

DARA. You are wrong, Prosecutor.

ROSHANARA (*unseen*). He's right!

DARA. Islam is the only path I walk, I just don't reject others.

PROSECUTOR *opens a book and reads.*

PROSECUTOR TALIB.
    'What shall I do? I know not what I am,
    I am neither Christian, nor Jew, nor heathen, nor a
        Muslim.'

PROSECUTOR *closes the book.*

SIPIHR. Where's the rest of the poem? That's not the end of the poem.

QAZI SAYED. Thank you, Prosecutor, if you have finished, I call upon Prince Dara Shikoh as Counsel for the Defence.

SIPIHR *struggles to stand up*.

SIPIHR. Your honour, I would like to be the Prince's defence.

QAZI SAYED. I beg your pardon, but you are his son?

SIPIHR. My father will not defend himself properly.

PROSECUTOR TALIB. Your honour...

SIPIHR. He is too honest.

PROSECUTOR TALIB. You cannot change the Counsel for the Defence in the middle of proceedings!

ROSHANARA (*unseen*). Sipihr is a prisoner!

QAZI SAYED. No, I don't believe we can...

DARA *addresses his sister behind the screen*.

DARA. Thank you, Roshanara, for your contribution.

QAZI SAYED (*to* SIPIHR). I understand you are a prisoner?

SIPIHR. So is my father but he is defending himself.

QAZI SAYED *is wavering. There is a knocking from behind the marble screen*.

PROSECUTOR TALIB. I think you had better get on with proceedings, your honour.

QAZI SAYED. Thank you, Prosecutor, I shall not be hurried in my own court.

SIPIHR. If my father is to be run through by his own sword, at the very least his complete verse should be read!

QAZI SAYED. I understand your request, Prince Sipihr.

PROSECUTOR TALIB. It's too late, I have finished my questioning.

SIPIHR. But –

QAZI SAYED (*interrupting*). Please remain seated and do not interrupt again.

SIPIHR *is put back in his place.*

Bring the Prince forward.

DARA *is brought forward, still in fetters.*

Can the Defence state the name of the accused.

DARA. Prince Dara Shikoh. See what I mean about the mechanics of ritual?

QAZI SAYED. Counsel for the Defence, would you like to start by reciting the remainder of your poem as part of your testimony?

DARA. I thank you, Qazi, though I fear we are beyond that.

SIPIHR. Say it, Father!

QAZI SAYED. Silence in court.

DARA. If my poem places me here, I am in brilliant company. Islam's most revered poets would be in the dock – Rumi, Ibni, Arabi...

SIPIHR. Speak the rest!

QAZI SAYED. Stop the boy crying out.

SIPIHR *is stifled.*

Proceed.

DARA. With respect, your honour, this whole trial is meaningless. You and I are both pawns, this is between my brother and myself. A boy who, aged fifteen, stood his ground in front of a raging elephant without so much as flinching. I have underestimated him, and I fear I am lost.

He fixes his gaze again on the women's screen.

Can you hear me, Aurangzeb?

QAZI SAYED. The Emperor is not present.

DARA. Oh but he is.

The court whispers, a ripple of energy running through them at the proceedings taking this unprecedented turn.

QAZI SAYED. Quieten down in court. (*To* DARA.) Your defence, please.

DARA (*to unseen* AURANGZEB). I know you are concealed, peeping through the lattice with our sister and the other women. I feel your eyes on me. The Prophet, may peace be upon him, never dreamed women would end up obscured behind screens, beneath veils... His wives needed privacy, their home was filled with people so, commensurate with his situation, he suggested the hijab.

QAZI SAYED. Is this relevant to the case?

DARA. Maybe, maybe not, for better or worse, I am my own counsel. I am trying to illustrate how the Prophet's circumstances, peace be upon him, are not ours. You see, Aurangzeb, all it was was that others wanted to emulate His wives, and why wouldn't they? Aisha, Zaynab, Safiyya... worthy, honourable women – wearing the veil made others feel like these chosen ones so the hijab was born. It became tradition, evolved through necessity, not God's thoughts, certainly not His instructions, and, Aurangzeb, some of these traditions you take as truths, are stifling.

PROSECUTOR TALIB. Apostasy!

DARA. And, what's more, brother, I've hated you for it. My heart has struggled to love you, as you have struggled to love me. But Allah is life!

QAZI SAYED. Really, I have to stop you, this is not some gathering of whirling dervishes –

DARA. Were we dervishes, we would whirl ourselves out of our heads and into our hearts, rendering these proceedings utterly redundant.

PROSECUTOR TALIB. Your honour, the Counsel is meandering, I cannot see –

DARA (*cutting him off*). Do you remember the tiger and the goat, Aurangzeb? Aurangzeb?

QAZI SAYED. I must stop you there, Counsel, you are straying from the point.

DARA. Have the decency to let me finish. Remember, Aurangzeb?

QAZI SAYED. Very well, proceed, but remember this is your one and only chance to save yourself and if you think the Emperor is listening to you, you are abused.

DARA. He would not miss this for the world.

Appealing to AURANGZEB, *brother to brother*.

Aurangzeb, remember how fascinated Grandfather was with animals? What he loved most in the world was alcohol, and creatures. He hunted, painted and devoured them. So when he heard about a goat living with a tiger in a cage, do you remember, he was captivated, and he had that goat removed? We all watched the tiger become disconsolate, pacing the cage, growling in anguish, day and night. Then Jahangir had another goat brought in, of a similar size and shape. The tiger approached the new goat, sniffed her, and promptly broke her neck, remember? We saw the broken goat being carried out, like a rag. Then Jahangir put in a sheep, which lasted minutes before being killed and consumed. Then finally the first goat was brought back, and… do you remember what happened? The tiger rolled over exposing its belly, the goat climbed on and let him lick its face till it shone.

The court is very quiet.

What did you think, Aurangzeb, when we were boys, did you think the tiger was weak and the goat deviant, or did you swell with gratitude knowing that in this world, against the odds, were tigers who loved goats and goats who loved tigers? That goat made the tiger's heart expand, it demanded it, who knows why, why that goat of all goats, was it more worthy than others, less goat-like? It was just how it was beheld. The tiger's heart was open to the goat.

Beat.

You know what that is, you once understood how it was for love to transcend boundaries…

There is shuffling from behind the screen.

Like the elephant and the blind men, where one finds a trunk, one an ear, the other a leg so they conclude that they each encountered an entirely different beast – did their blindness make the elephant not an elephant, Aurangzeb? Love exists, possibility exists, harmony exists, and if we weren't blind we would see it. You and I, Aurangzeb, as Rumi says, are like boats dashing together, our eyes are darkened yet we are in clear water. It is unnecessary. Love is possible.

Beat.

Brother, all I ask is that you show mercy to my sons.

There is a knock on the screen and a male voice is heard.

AURANGZEB (*from behind the screen*). Close proceedings.

QAZI SAYED *is surprised, he immediately draws things to a close.*

QAZI SAYED. That's enough from the Counsel, now, put the fetters back on.

DARA. Aurangzeb? I shouldn't have fought, I didn't want to.

DARA *is put back in to foot fetters.*

Can you forgive me, brother? In the twenty mentions of apostasy in the Quran, not one prescribes the death penalty.

PROSECUTOR TALIB. Which Quran do you read?

DARA. The Hadiths do, but they are not the Quran – was Abdullah a prophet?

QAZI SAYED. That's enough now.

DARA. How did those Hadiths grow more powerful than Allah? They were men, Aurangzeb… please…

He struggles to make his point.

Not gods.

PROSECUTOR TALIB. Gods, plural, your honour, do you hear that?

DARA. Allah deals with apostasy in the next world, you can rest assured that if I were an apostate I will be dealt with in the hereafter, but I am no such thing!

QAZI SAYED. Prepare the accused for sentencing.

DARA (*shouts up to the grate*). There is no God but Allah and Muhammad was his messenger!

QAZI SAYED. Prince Dara, stop now, enough, stop. Take the boy out!

SIPIHR. Father…

SIPIHR stands, trying to reach out to his father. He is taken out. DARA *shouts up to* AURANGZEB *in the gallery.*

DARA. If you kill me, brother, I forgive you, but I ask with all my heart, do not murder my sons!

There is a clattering as AURANGZEB *vacates his position behind the screens.* DARA *tracks his course.* AURANGZEB *emerges, the* QAZI *looks shocked to see him and speeds up his verdict.*

QAZI SAYED. The courtroom here today finds Prince Dara Shikoh guilty as accused, of apostasy and as such, is sentenced to death.

DARA. But you can save me, brother.

For a moment, the brothers face each other, eye to eye, before AURANGZEB *leaves the courtroom with a bang.*

Interval.

ACT FOUR

Scene One

The past.

MIAN MIR*'s house in Lahore.* MIAN MIR *is seated on the ground with several people around him. Some* DISCIPLES *are posted at his gates.* DARA (*early twenties*) *approaches and goes straight to the front of a small queue.*

JAMAL. You need to join the back of the queue, sir.

    DARA *is taken aback.*

DARA. You need to learn some respect.

JAMAL. We have equal respect for everybody.

DARA. I am here for the Sufi saint, Mian Mir's, blessing.

JAMAL. And he will be happy to see you, sir, but would you be so kind as to wait behind this lady?

    DARA *takes* JAMAL *to one side.*

DARA. I have travelled from Agra especially, I am Prince Dara.

JAMAL. He is currently engaged with others, Prince, but time will pass and then he will see you, Mian Mir turns nobody away.

    The SECOND DISCIPLE *speaks to the person at the head of the queue.*

SECOND DISCIPLE. Mian Mir will see you now, sir.

    DARA *speaks to* JAMAL.

DARA. What is your name?

JAMAL. Mine? Jamal.

DARA. Jamal, I don't appreciate your attitude.

JAMAL. Sir –

DARA. Prince.

JAMAL. Prince, this is a sacred place, everybody is treated alike.

DARA. That's right, a place of devotion, I am not here to be aggravated.

JAMAL. Of course you're not, sir, I mean, Prince…

Two people leave MIAN MIR*'s room. The* SECOND DISCIPLE *speaks to* DARA *and the lady in front.*

SECOND DISCIPLE. Mian Mir will see you both now.

JAMAL. Please, go in.

DARA. Thank you.

He goes in, irate. He isn't sure which one is MIAN MIR. *Finally he works it out, approaches* MIAN MIR, *bows respectfully, speaks in a low voice.*

Master Mian Mir. Your guards have been heavy-handed with me.

MIAN MIR. They used violence?

DARA. I don't mean physically.

MIAN MIR. Did they call you names, spit at you?

DARA *is silent.*

So you are a somebody in this world?

DARA. My name is Dara, I am Shah Jahan's eldest son.

MIAN MIR. Prince Dara, I have no guards, only friends who help ensure that equality takes place outside my home as well as in. If my friends were not protecting this, imagine? You might have walked directly in front of other visitors.

DARA. Mian Mir, it is awkward for me to stay on the street, I am in constant danger of being recognised.

MIAN MIR. And recognition is an impediment?

DARA. I have very little time before I must return to Agra. I came especially for your blessing. This is not how I would have wished our first meeting to go.

MIAN MIR. You want my blessing?

DARA. Please, Master Mian Mir. You've probably heard I am about to leave on an assignment to the south?

MIAN MIR. Expanding the Empire?

DARA. Yes.

MIAN MIR. So you'll have the chance to slaughter lots of people?

DARA. I hope not.

MIAN MIR. But this is your undertaking, surely you have to kill in the pursuit of more land?

DARA. I have been ordered to quell a rebellion. That duty falls to me.

MIAN MIR. Oh, so no killing then?

DARA *is silent.*

What is it you want?

DARA. Your blessing.

MIAN MIR. For war?

DARA. I came here on my own without men and you laugh at me.

An OLD WOMAN *comes forward with a rupee.* MIAN MIR *speaks to her.*

MIAN MIR. Look around the room, who is the poorest? Give your rupee to whoever needs it the most.

She offers it around, everybody refuses.

There must be somebody? The Prince, perhaps, why not give it to Prince Dara. He has a whole Empire yet he wants more. Not content with his own realm, he sets out to take somebody else's.

DARA. Mian Mir.

MIAN MIR. Or maybe I should have the rupee?

DARA *gets up and leaves.* MIAN MIR *laughs and claps, the others in the room are infected with his joy, they giggle too.*

OLD WOMAN. Poor boy.

MIAN MIR. He will be back.

DARA *returns. He enters the room and puts his head on* MIAN MIR*'s foot. He leaves it there for a long time.*

(*To* DARA.) You came for your rupee?

DARA. *Astaghfirullah.* I apologise for my behaviour, I was wrong to get cross with your disciples, I am calm now. I leave tomorrow with a full army and I humbly ask for your protection before I lead so many men away from homes and families.

MIAN MIR *doesn't say anything.*

What can I say, Mian Mir? My behaviour was presumptuous and disrespectful, I thank you for your lesson.

MIAN MIR. I'm sorry, what did you want?

DARA. Your blessing, Mian Mir…

MIAN MIR. You have it.

DARA *is a bit put out.*

DARA. Do you have any advice for me?

MIAN MIR. No.

DARA. I've not been able to sleep.

MIAN MIR. Take something.

DARA. I am thirsty for answers, Mian Mir.

MIAN MIR. More, always more. I don't have any answers.

DARA. I know, because I feel, I cannot go to war without your blessing.

MIAN MIR. I fear you see the world in miniature, Prince Dara, on this scale, as if it were painted by one of your royal painters.

He indicates the size of a miniature painting.

With his brushes plucked from squirrels' tails, and paints in tiny disused shells, yet you think your picture is the entire universe. You want water?

(*To one of his* DISCIPLES.) Bring some water.

(*To everybody*.) Sit.

DARA *sits.* MIAN MIR *does not speak directly to* DARA *but to the assembled people.*

Once there was an Emperor in the desert who was cut off from his army. His enemies were getting close to him and so he runs, this Emperor, runs and runs, but you know what the desert is like, you cannot run because you sweat and lose water. But he must run because he is being chased by his enemy. All he has with him now is five men. They have given him all their food and all their water so now they are dying, they cannot keep up with his running, so they stop and one by one end their lives just where they are. From five there are four, then three, then two and finally the last man dies. Now it is only the Emperor in this wide expanse of desert. It is so hot and it is a great distance to the nearest village. The Emperor is on the sand, crawling painfully away from the encroaching enemy, but he can barely move. Within the hour, he will be dead too, from dehydration or else his enemy will capture and kill him. He cannot swallow, he cannot think, he is parchment. Another hour goes by and really he is on his very final thread of life, a moth in its final thrust. But out of nowhere, in these penultimate seconds, a man appears, carrying something. What do you think it is? It is a glass of water. He speaks to the Emperor, he says, 'If you drink this water, you will have enough strength to get to the village, the enemy will not chase you. At this village, you can eat and drink all you need, your life will be saved, but in return, I take your kingdom, every piece of it, your palaces, your people, your priceless jewels… what do you say, Emperor, would you like this water?'

Beat.

What do you think the Emperor does?

DARA. Takes the water.

DARA *speaks loudly, intuitively, as if there was no one else in the room.*

MIAN MIR. Of course.

DARA. He takes the water.

MIAN MIR. He takes the water. So how much is his kingdom worth, that he would exchange it all for a glass of water? Nothing, am I right? All right, I am tired.

MIAN MIR *gets up, goes towards* DARA. DARA *weeps, a clean burst of tears.* MIAN MIR *brings* DARA *to his feet and places a hand on* DARA*'s heart, then takes* DARA*'s hand and puts it on his own heart, his hand on top of* DARA*'s. He looks in to* DARA*'s eyes.*

With my blessing, go.

Scene Two

The past.

HIRA BAI, *whom we have seen glimpses of before, is young and real. She teases* AURANGZEB *(early thirties).*

HIRA BAI. Who's this?

She throws herself on the floor in a dead faint.

AURANGZEB. Stop it.

HIRA BAI. Who is it?

AURANGZEB. I'm not talking to you.

They are deeply in love. She hums, breaking into full singing, while she mimes herself stretching up to pluck a mango off a tree. Still singing, though laughter threatens to break through, she mimes AURANGZEB *seeing her as if struck by lightning, then collapsing to the ground. He comes and tickles her, interrupting her mime.*

HIRA BAI. No, don't!

AURANGZEB. You are a wicked djinn who stole all my sense!

HIRA BAI. Do you only love me because you've lost your mind?

AURANGZEB. Who says I love you?

HIRA BAI. You didn't faint when you first saw me?

AURANGZEB. I tripped and fell.

HIRA BAI. It was the glare of the sun, the exhausting walk round your aunt's garden that turned your legs to soup...

AURANGZEB. I swooned at your hideousness.

She jumps on him. They are physical and playful with one another.

HIRA BAI. Which is precisely why you hounded your aunt to trade me for a harem girl, Prince of Poise and Self-Possession... extracting me from her husband's harem...

AURANGZEB. He should have paid me to take you.

HIRA BAI. A horrible Hindu girl like me.

AURANGZEB. With your dry hair and mean eyes…

HIRA BAI. Better not look then, just taste.

They kiss, her hands covering his eyes.

AURANGZEB. Can you hear the blood thundering in my veins? How did you tangle me so, Hira? I forget everything when I'm with you…

HIRA BAI. Do you know what else will make you forget?

AURANGZEB. What?

HIRA BAI. Wine.

AURANGZEB. Wine?

HIRA BAI. Let's drink some wine.

AURANGZEB *is speechless.*

Let's try, a sip, just one.

She gets some wine.

AURANGZEB. What are you doing?

HIRA BAI. It smells nice.

She takes a sip.

AURANGZEB. Why are you doing this?

HIRA BAI. Seeing if you love me or not.

She offers him the goblet.

AURANGZEB. Hira, I would do anything for you…

HIRA BAI. Then, drink some wine.

AURANGZEB. How does drinking wine prove my love?

HIRA BAI. Because you detest it so.

He looks at her.

AURANGZEB. I have never tasted alcohol in my life.

HIRA BAI. Why don't you taste it now?

AURANGZEB. You lead me further and further from myself...

He takes the goblet and goes to drink from it.

HIRA BAI. That's enough, Aurangzeb!

She seizes it from him. He looks at her.

I wanted to test your love, my love, not corrupt you with unlucky liquor!

AURANGZEB. You don't need to test me, I don't want to be anywhere but with you.

HIRA BAI. Then stay, always stay.

They are ruffled by their near-miss.

I can't lead you from yourself, Aurangzeb, you are too strong for that, my sober sweetheart.

AURANGZEB. I come from a line of inebriates.

HIRA BAI. Your father?

AURANGZEB. Grandfather. Father quelled it. On marrying my mother, he emptied his entire wine cellar into the river. Though wine's not all he pours away.

HIRA BAI. What would you be like as Emperor?

AURANGZEB. It would never happen.

HIRA BAI. Imagine it did?

They laugh.

How would your Empire look?

AURANGZEB. Calm. Like a mosque. Ordered, safe, a place for everything.

HIRA BAI. That sounds boring...

He tickles her again.

Most of your Empire is Hindu!

AURANGZEB. They'd chose Islam, eventually, its power, its purity, they'd want that serenity.

HIRA BAI. You're not so serene with me...

AURANGZEB. Because you, Hira, are my greatest jihad.

HIRA BAI. What's jihad?

AURANGZEB. A struggle with the lower self.

HIRA BAI. We are like two animals who shouldn't really be together.

AURANGZEB. What am I, a snake?

HIRA BAI. No! You're a tiger.

He growls accordingly.

AURANGZEB. And you are a –

HIRA BAI (*interrupting*). Goat!

AURANGZEB. What if you became Muslim, Hira?

HIRA BAI. It would make me sad. My family are Hindu, it's who I am.

AURANGZEB. I would have drunk that wine for you.

HIRA BAI. What if you became Hindu?

She smiles a wicked smile.

AURANGZEB. I told you, you are my all-consuming, ravishing jihad.

Scene Three

The past.

DARA (*twenties*) *and* SHAH JAHAN, *in his prime, are in the middle of a heated debate.*

SHAH JAHAN. Being a prince is what you are born to be!

DARA. Why would a drop become a pearl when it could join the ocean?

SHAH JAHAN. What are you saying, son?

DARA. Our spiritual search is what we are born to, Father. Why are we so privileged? I cannot live with it!

SHAH JAHAN. We have obligations beyond other people's wildest dreams, huge weights of responsibility, privilege is a percentage of how we live, a part.

DARA. I want to be a faqir, I don't want to be draped in pearls the size of pigeon's eggs.

SHAH JAHAN. These are my prayer beads!

DARA. I'm not talking about you, I'm talking about me, Father, all I want is to be close to Allah.

SHAH JAHAN. You are my Crown Prince.

DARA. You have other sons! How do you ignore the fact that the Prophet, peace be upon him, slept on the floor yet we Islamic rulers sit on golden thrones? The Sufis stay true to Him, they give everything away. But when I give the shirt off my back to a man who needs it, before I know it another one grows on me, with golden threads, imbedded with jewels. I am not allowed to reduce myself to nothing, it is not right!

SHAH JAHAN. Dara, who will rule when I'm gone if not you?

DARA. I won't make a good Emperor, I don't want... power.

SHAH JAHAN. You have intelligence, compassion, not a lazy bone in your body, you are shrewd, brave and peace-loving, Dara, you are perfect!

DARA. But, Father, I lack the appetite for it. Sufis love, emperors kill.

SHAH JAHAN. Not always, not all of them, not you, Dara.

DARA. How do you know that?

SHAH JAHAN. Because I can see how you would rule, you know it too.

DARA. Part of me wants it, of course, but so much of me questions it, Father. I don't think an Emperor is who I am.

SHAH JAHAN. Tell me your vision, what do you dream of?

DARA. I long to be at one with my universe.

SHAH JAHAN. So unify Hindustan.

DARA *is silent.*

Being a faqir is not an option, we shall not speak of this again.

DARA. But, Father, my heart –

SHAH JAHAN *is fierce and conclusive.*

SHAH JAHAN. Is mine, do you understand? I am your father, you are a branch of my tree, to prune, nurture or amputate as I decree.

Scene Four

The past.

HIRA BAI *is very sick with consumption. She is too weak to do Wudu.* AURANGZEB *washes her.*

AURANGZEB. Every project, major or small, we think of God, *bismillah.*

HIRA BAI (*whispered*). *Bismillah.*

AURANGZEB *reminds her how it goes.*

AURANGZEB. Hands.

Swish and spit.

HIRA BAI *can hardly speak.*

HIRA BAI. Three times.

AURANGZEB. Nose... you don't have to do the nose today, Hira...

She smiles weakly.

Spread your hands, ear to ear, hairline to chin, three times... wrists to elbows, fore and back arms –

HIRA BAI *rasps a last breath.*

Hira? Hira?

She doesn't respond. He tries to rouse her, he grows desperate.

Ya Allah, Ya Allah, Ya Allah.

He picks her up, she is like a rag doll.

God wouldn't give you to me in order to take you away... He would have made me far, far stronger than I am, or I will break. Hira?

All my childhood, throughout my marriages, on the road with my soldiers... You are the only person who liked me, honestly, without effort. I was alone until I met you, Hira. Hira!

He looks at HIRA BAI.

Is it the Angel of Death, already?

He speaks to God. A new intention comes into him.

Thank you, Allah, for your lesson, forgive your sinful servant, I will never again lose myself. I never missed a prayer, but I did desert my duty, my family, for my goat, and now I am wretched. Use me, give me back my heart, mighty Allah, and I shall protect it, accept me as your ultimate servant, I am yours, all yours.

Scene Five

1659. AURANGZEB *and* DARA *face each other for a moment as at the end of the trial.* AURANGZEB *goes.* DARA *is in his prison cell.* DARA *and* SIPIHR *await news.*

SIPIHR. You should have said the rest of the poem.

DARA. Don't tell me what I should and shouldn't do, Sipihr.

SIPIHR. It spoke against you, out of context.

DARA. The context itself was what was wrong. I tried, Sipihr.

SIPIHR. I know.

Beat.

DARA. I saw you struggling with your prayers, you must pray, son.

SIPIHR. Today I couldn't.

DARA. What do you mean you couldn't?

SIPIHR. I just couldn't.

DARA. What's wrong with you?

SIPIHR. Father, let's not argue…

DARA. Whatever happens in your life, you cannot dismiss Salat!

SIPIHR. They could come for you before dawn!

DARA *backs down.*

DARA. Your mother wouldn't like us to argue, would she?

DARA *extends his hands to* SIPIHR.

Friends?

SIPIHR. They kept your ring.

DARA. One day we're emperors, the next we're prisoners, that's how it goes.

SIPIHR. What do they want with it?

DARA. God makes us no promises. Nor does He expect much in return. When they asked the Prophet, peace be upon him, which was the best part of Islam, do you know what he answered?

SIPIHR. I don't think so.

DARA. 'To offer food and say salaam to those you know and those you don't.' That is all He really asks.

SIPIHR. I worry sometimes that I don't know God well.

DARA. Offer him food, say hello.

SIPIHR *smiles.*

We are all full of doubts, Sipihr, whether we admit them or not, Allah knows.

SIPIHR *recites* DARA*'s poem to him.*

SIPIHR.
    'What shall I do? I know not what I am,
    I am neither Christian nor Jew nor heathen nor a
       Muslim...'

DARA. We shouldn't be afraid of questions.

SIPIHR.

>'I am neither of the east nor of the west,
>Neither of the earth nor of the ocean…'

DARA.

>'Nature's mint I am not, nor the all-encompassing sky's,
>I am not composed of earth, water, air or fire,
>I am neither the dead clay nor the illuminating brilliance,
>I am not from this world nor from that,
>Not from Heaven nor from Hell,
>I am neither my body nor even my self for I am my Lord's self.
>Only Him I search, only Him I know,
>Only Him I see and only Him I call,
>He is the beginning and the end,
>He is within and He is beyond.'

Beat.

Sipihr?

SIPIHR. Yes, Father?

DARA. Tonight, would you call me Baba?

Scene Six

1659, Red Fort, Delhi. IMPERIAL SERVANTS *are crouching, cleaning the tiles, it is the evening after* DARA*'s trial, lamps shine behind water refracting the light. Lively music is played,* ROSHANARA *smokes her hookah. She forces one of her male* SERVANTS *to dance with her.*

ROSHANARA. Dance with me, Akhtar, dance!

ITBAR, *holding a letter, comes in with* AURANGZEB.

Brother, Itbar, join us!

AURANGZEB. What are you doing, Roshanara?

ROSHANARA. Having a party. We did it, Aurangzeb, Dara will be dead by morning!

AURANGZEB. A Prince of the Empire has been found guilty of apostasy, Roshanara – it's not an occasion for dancing or singing.

ROSHANARA. They are joyous, Aurangzeb, giving thanks to Allah that Dara is defeated.

AURANGZEB (*violently to the* MUSICIANS). Stop your racket!

They stop playing.

(*To* ROSHANARA.) You are a bloodthirsty hound. There are ways to express joy which are godly.

ROSHANARA. Such as?

AURANGZEB. Feed a mendicant, give more zakat. Imad?

IMAD *is there.*

Make sure they don't start again. Ever.

IMAD. Certainly, Sire.

AURANGZEB. That's an instruction throughout the city, no more music.

IMAD. Sire?

AURANGZEB. Burn the instruments, do as I say. What do people think, that we were given lives to fritter them away? I am in earnest. Close down the drum rooms, sack the drummers, burn the drums.

ROSHANARA. Have you lost your mind, Aurangzeb?

AURANGZEB. And the girls, all dancing girls must get themselves a husband before Friday or they will be thrown in the river, understand?

IMAD *hurries the* MUSICIANS *out.*

ROSHANARA. The choice is coffin or throne, brother, not both together, not live in a coffin while on the throne!

AURANGZEB. Enough is enough. (*To* AKHTAR.) There is a troop of monkeys in the courtyard, shoo them away! Your bloodlust disgusts me, Roshanara, enough to go right now and liberate our brother.

ROSHANARA. But –

AURANGZEB. Who have you become? Leave us.

She goes. The two men are left on their own. After a silence, AURANGZEB *speaks.*

Should I spare him, Itbar?

ITBAR. How can I advise, Sire?

AURANGZEB. How can anyone?

ITBAR. Prince Dara is your brother. But my experience of family is limited, I was separated from mine at a young age…

AURANGZEB. Something is on your mind, speak.

ITBAR. Many things, Sire, but for one, if I may, the musicians. Their families have been artists in this country for hundreds of years. Some of your mullahs only came from Persia as little as fifteen years ago…

AURANGZEB. But India belongs to us now, Itbar.

ITBAR. Of course, Sire.

AURANGZEB. To Allah. Read me the letter.

ITBAR (*reading*). 'Son, accept my gift of fruit with my greatest respect.'

AURANGZEB. Not affection, notice. Go on.

ITBAR (*reading*). 'I take responsibility for this war of succession, I acknowledge my failings as a father and urge you to accept my most profound apologies. I must ask you now, Aurangzeb, with the wisdom of hindsight over the actions I myself took, to spare Dara's life.'

AURANGZEB. There we have it.

ITBAR. 'I vow to force allies loyal to Dara to desist from any adventure. Give him a house, a handful of servants, let him live.'

AURANGZEB. Prepared to sacrifice his own dignity, bleating Dara's cause as ever. Family.

He is clearly conflicted.

(*To* ITBAR.) I want no more of these letters, stop his ink and paper supply, however much he pleads.

ITBAR *bows.* IMAD *comes back in.*

IMAD. Forgive me for interrupting, Your Majesty…

AURANGZEB. What is it, Imad?

IMAD. Two visitors just arrived, by foot. They walked all the way up especially to ask for Itbar.

AURANGZEB. Are you expecting anybody?

ITBAR. No, Sire.

IMAD. It is definitely you they want.

ITBAR. How did they know I was here?

AURANGZEB. Bring them in.

ITBAR. That is not necessary, Sire…

IMAD *bows, goes.*

AURANGZEB (*to* ITBAR). I prize your fidelity, Itbar, I did not know you had friends beyond the palace walls.

ITBAR. I do not, Sire, my work is my life.

IMAD *returns with an impoverished elderly couple, they bow deeply.*

AURANGZEB. State the purpose of your visit.

ITBAR'S MOTHER. Is that really you?

ITBAR. I do not know this lady, Sire.

ITBAR'S MOTHER. Standing with the Emperor.

ITBAR. Nor this gentlemen.

ITBAR'S MOTHER. I am your mother, Itbar. We are your parents.

AURANGZEB (*to a* SERVANT). Bring tea for Itbar's relatives.

AURANGZEB *watches with interest,* IMAD *with discomfort.* ITBAR'S MOTHER *almost whispers to* ITBAR, *embarrassed to speak in front of the Emperor.*

ITBAR'S MOTHER. We hoped you had a chance but look how you've turned out!

ITBAR. I last saw you when I was eleven.

ITBAR'S MOTHER. I know, son, I never forgot.

ITBAR. 'Take him, go on, take him', are the last words I heard you say.

ITBAR'S FATHER. Son, you must understand our situation…

ITBAR. How dare you come to my place of work parading the scraps of your love.

The scene has drawn others to the hall. ROSHANARA *loiters, captured by the unfolding scene.*

ITBAR'S MOTHER. We're not here for money, son...

ITBAR. You sold me into slavery.

ITBAR'S MOTHER. We were desperate.

ITBAR. And my new owners fed me opium and cut off my genitals.

ITBAR'S FATHER. Son, please...

ITBAR. I'm sorry, do I embarrass you? Pressed a rag soaked in boiled oil on my wounds, covered the rag in earth and put me to bed for forty days.

ITBAR'S MOTHER. I can't bear to listen to this...

ITBAR. Two out of twelve of us survived from that batch and went on to Imperial careers, no matter that I cannot expel urine like a man nor like a woman, I'm embarrassing you again, my apologies. If they named me as they name their other slaves, I would not be honey-scented or fat-pretty-one but half-a-man. You come now wanting recompense having poisoned the roots of my life. Imad? Imad!

IMAD *doesn't know what to do.*

Take these two to the whipping post, tell the boys twenty lashes each.

ITBAR'S MOTHER. No, Itbar!

ITBAR'S FATHER. You cannot whip your mother, Itbar!

ROSHANARA *is moved by* ITBAR*'s story.*

ROSHANARA. Itbar, I'll take them.

IMAD *leaves.* ITBAR *pursues his parents.*

ITBAR. I will give you the rupees I earn from selling the dung from my elephants, nothing more, and if you ever come near me again, here or in Agra, I will kill you.

ROSHANARA. This way.

ROSHANARA *takes the parents off.* ITBAR *excuses himself from* AURANGZEB.

ITBAR. Excuse me, Sire.

AURANGZEB. Of course.

>ITBAR *heads off.* AURANGZEB *calls him back.*

>Itbar?

ITBAR. Yes, Sire?

AURANGZEB. I need to talk to you about something.

Scene Seven

1659, DARA*'s cell.* ITBAR *appears at the door with a* PRISON GUARD *and another man. The Prison Warden,* HUSSAIN, *comes up behind the* GUARD.

HUSSAIN. What's happening?

GUARD. None of your business.

HUSSAIN. Who are these visitors?

>ITBAR *comes in with the other man.*

SIPIHR. Itbar, is that you?

ITBAR. Good evening, Master Sipihr – (*To* DARA.) Prince.

>DARA *stands.*

DARA. Is it that bad that I have lost my name, Itbar?

ITBAR. I'm afraid so, Sire.

DARA. No brotherly reprieve?

>*The other man comes forward, he is the* EXECUTIONER. *He expertly bundles a hood over* DARA*'s head.* SIPIHR *fights, so does* DARA.

SIPIHR. Give me a sword, give me a sword!

He attacks the EXECUTIONER *with his bare hands, the* GUARD *and* ITBAR *hold him back.*

DARA. Show me the way, my Prophets and Saints, Lord, God, Allah...

SIPIHR. You will burn in the fires of Hell, all of you!

ITBAR (*to the* EXECUTIONER). The Emperor does not want to know where the body is buried, an unmarked grave, understood?

EXECUTIONER. Yes, sir.

The EXECUTIONER *unsheathes a massive sword.*

SIPIHR. Baba!

Scene Eight

The ghost of HIRA BAI *sings.* SHAH JAHAN *and* JAHANARA *are in their prison quarters. It is dawn, they have been up all night.* ITBAR *arrives with a large box.*

JAHANARA. You're back, what news?

ITBAR. I have a parcel from the Emperor.

JAHANARA. Baba, do you hear, Aurangzeb has sent us something?

SHAH JAHAN. A gift, my letter worked, he has saved him!

JAHANARA. Has he, Itbar, is Dara safe?

SHAH JAHAN. Has he sent a letter, Itbar? Oh, it's heavy.

He tries lifting the box.

JAHANARA. Itbar?

ITBAR *doesn't answer.*

SHAH JAHAN. I think it's watermelon, Jahanara, from Afghanistan maybe, or Iran, it's too heavy for mangoes. It is extremely heavy, maybe it's both, watermelon and mangoes?

JAHANARA. Is there no letter there?

SHAH JAHAN. Do you remember how I used to call Dara my watermelon? I can't see a thing, Jahanara.

She looks in the box. She immediately retches.

JAHANARA. Take your hands out, Baba!

SHAH JAHAN. What's wrong, Jahanara?

She cannot help but cry and retch. SHAH JAHAN *opens the box again and peers in, his head right in the box. He leaps back.*

Forgive him, oh God, forgive him, forgive him.

How do I still smell apples?

AFIA *runs in, alerted by the noise.*

AFIA. Itbar?

AFIA *takes in the scene and looks at* ITBAR.

What did you do, what did you bring them?

ITBAR *leaves,* AFIA *follows.*

Don't shake me off!

She seizes him.

What have you done?

ITBAR. I let you down, Afia.

AFIA. No…

ITBAR. You know the poem in the water garden?

AFIA. On the wall?

JAHANARA *calls from the room.*

JAHANARA. Afia?

ITBAR. 'If there be paradise on earth, it is this, it is this, it is this'...

JAHANARA. Afia!

AFIA *urges* ITBAR.

AFIA. Wait for me, don't go anywhere...

JAHANARA. Afia...

ITBAR. They need you, go.

AFIA. Itbar!

ITBAR. I'll wait.

AFIA. Promise?

ITBAR. Promise.

She goes back to JAHANARA *and* SHAH JAHAN. ITBAR *unwinds the scarf from around his jacket and makes it into a noose. He searches above his head for something to hang it on. He finds it.* HIRA BAI *sings.*

ACT FIVE

Scene One

A week later. The call to prayer sounds, bold and beautiful. It is
DARA *singing. The two voices,* DARA*'s and* HIRA BAI*'s,*
weave around each other, each holding their own.
AURANGZEB *returns from Friday prayers at the big mosque,*
with his retinue. The FAQIR *sits on the steps.*

AURANGZEB. Move the Faqir off.

> IMAD *approaches the* FAQIR.

IMAD. Get along there, the Emperor is coming.

FAQIR. That's why I'm here.

MULLAH FAROOQ. You are deluded if you think he will
converse with a half-naked heathen.

FAQIR. Are you so dense as to not yet understand that we are
brothers?

> MULLAH FAROOQ *scoffs.*

We are carved from the same wood, you and I, Mullah.

MULLAH FAROOQ. Your religion bears no relation to mine.

FAQIR. Sufism is the kernel of Islam, the inner Islam, we
radiate out from the Prophet, may peace be upon him. You
cannot shake a brother off, however you'd like to, siblings
are siblings.

> *The* MULLAH *gives his stick to* IMAD, *for him to use it on*
> *the* FAQIR. IMAD *is compromised.*

Hit out, why don't you, religious man?

> AURANGZEB *joins them.*

AURANGZEB. I know this character.

FAQIR. Emperor, we meet again.

AURANGZEB. He's a squalid, filthy liar.

FAQIR. Your self-loathing is as acute as it was on the first day of our acquaintance. I should have let your father take my life that day, instead of play my part in who you've become.

AURANGZEB. How dare you place your unclothed body at the foot of this mosque.

FAQIR. Built by your poor father, Aurangzeb.

AURANGZEB. Cover yourself up!

FAQIR. The innocent go naked. You think you can obscure yourself, beneath those clothes.

AURANGZEB. Public nudity breaks the law, take him in.

FAQIR. Better tell babies to be born fully dressed then, Emperor, make the animals wear hijab –

AURANGZEB (*interrupting*). Take him to the fort.

FAQIR. Hide the faces of the flowers –

AURANGZEB (*interrupting*). Put him in the dungeons –

FAQIR. You destroy our dargahs, you behead our princes...

AURANGZEB. Stop him speaking, put the blanket on his head!

FAQIR (*continuing*). And yet you speak our transcendent words five times a day. Careful with that blanket, it's covering his nakedness.

IMAD *lifts the* FAQIR*'s blanket up.* AURANGZEB *immediately stumbles,* IMAD *drops it again.*

I see you see them, Aurangzeb, some already gone, some to come. I warned you. My nudity hides your brazenness.

As FAQIR *speaks, ghosts from* AURANGZEB*'s past are released. They stand, clustered, to haunt him, some we know, some we don't.* MURAD, ITBAR...

Baby brother Murad, poisoned in prison, Itbar, whose soul you fouled with the task you set him, kept out of paradise by Allah – as we are told in the Quran, every suicide burns in Hell's fire for ever... Your nephew, Sipihr, still in your dungeons, but you know that young man's fate already, don't you? Your brother, Dara, whose head you sent in a box. It's your shame beneath this blanket, Emperor.

AURANGZEB. Prepare a case of apostasy against him.

FAQIR. Apostasy, am I to be killed as a non-believer?

FAQIR *laughs at this ludicrous notion, he speaks to Allah through* AURANGZEB.

And yet I see through it, Allah, whatever disguise you take, my love, my God, I recognise you still.

He is hauled off. HIRA BAI *gently joins the flock of dead.*

AURANGZEB. That's enough, we must clean this city up, we will not sit, exposed, on the mosque steps, we will be simple and humble, all. We will purge this Empire of its vices, stifle the creature within. Round up the liquor-sellers, cut their hands and feet off if they've not stopped selling within a month. Tell the Imperial gardeners to plant no more rose beds. Ban the use of silk, cotton, only cotton.

AURANGZEB *becomes more frantic, firing instructions to his men.*

All those dargahs, ban women from going inside, it invites lasciviousness. We must tax all non-Muslims, we will force conversions. I will bring this situation under Aurangzeb's control, you cannot lead if you do not kill! I am Allah's servant and nothing will stand in the way of my humble, loving design.

Scene Two

A jump forward in time.

It is 1707. The ghosts are gathered like a flock of birds, hovering close to AURANGZEB. *The* FAQIR *has joined them,* HIRA BAI *is there.* AURANGZEB *ages in front of us. He is eighty-nine years old. He is sick, his back is bent.* KAM, AURANGZEB*'s youngest son, and* AZAM, *his spirited third son, appear in his tent.*

KAM. How are you, Father?

AURANGZEB. Fighting fit. I need your agreement, boys, you won't leave this place until I have it.

KAM. Of course, Father.

AURANGZEB. Azam?

AZAM. I am your servant, Father.

AURANGZEB. You, Azam, I need you to go to Bijapur.

AZAM. Bijapur?

AURANGZEB. And Kam, you must go to Malwa. Whatever affairs you have, keep some men behind to settle your business, you'll go straight away tonight, understood?

KAM. Malwa?

AZAM. Complain if you will, you'll be there in two weeks, I've just been told to travel hundreds of miles!

AURANGZEB. Do not grieve me, Azam, you've given your word.

AZAM. I can't pretend I don't regret it now.

AURANGZEB. It is better this way.

AZAM. Better than what?

AURANGZEB. Your tongue is sharp, Azam, and your thoughts are sharper. There are seventeen of you Princes of eligible age. Great-grandson Farrukhsiyar is twenty-two already!

KAM. You will outlive us all, Father.

AZAM. Eighty-nine and going strong.

AURANGZEB. Hear me clearly, I do not want to see either of you again. Take your men, make a sound life.

AZAM. And who will rule after you, Father?

KAM draws his sword at the audacity of his brother's challenge.

AURANGZEB. No! Put your sword away, I will not have fighting at my bedside, brother pitched against brother, it is ungodly! Keep distance between you, I need your word.

The boys are silent.

Promise me?

KAM *and* AZAM. I promise.

AURANGZEB. Don't fall foul, boys. The art of reigning is so delicate that a king's jealousy can be aroused by a brother, or his shadow, even.

AZAM. Who is your shadow, Father?

AURANGZEB. I will not be drawn, Azam.

AZAM. Then I will leave you to your favourite, I have a colossal journey ahead.

AZAM bows deeply, kisses his father's hand.

Goodbye, brother, till we meet again.

KAM. Insha'Allah.

He takes his leave. There is silence between father and son.

AURANGZEB. I know not who I am, nor what I do.

KAM. Don't say so, Father.

AURANGZEB. I have not the least liking for this deceitful, weary world.

KAM. God loves patience, Father, and you are its embodiment. You've always told me, patience is a shield where Allah writes, 'victory', in invisible ink.

AURANGZEB. Afflicted with my maladies, not mentioning the anxieties, it's true that endurance has become habitual, but, Kam, it is not enough. My doggedness has not tamed the Marathas.

KAM. Are they tameable?

AURANGZEB. The Empire is suffering. She has become unwieldy, our Hindustan – I strayed far from my seat of power. Money is spent on the wrong things, Kam. Do you know I owe some of my soldiers fourteen months' wages? I may as well have built mausoleums! Even the men of Mecca expect bribes these days, because I bribed them once, twice... I thought it right to do these things, I misread Allah's signs.

KAM. Of course you didn't, Father.

AURANGZEB. In my purse you will find three hundred and five rupees from the proceeds of the caps I crochet and sell. Use this, not state money, bury this wanderer without fuss, Kam, my head bare. And then, hear me, distribute whatever is left of my rupees to the faqirs.

KAM. But you hate faqirs?

AURANGZEB. Hatred softens. We come with nothing into this world, but I go with a whole caravan of sins. What is it all for, Kam, do we live to merely consume a quantity of water and fodder?

KAM. And rule enormous Empires!

AURANGZEB. So long as there is breath in me I am driven to serve it, I find no release from labour.

KAM. You are the champion of Islam in Hindustan, Father.

AURANGZEB. But, Kam, after me comes chaos – seventeen Princes! Son, may I ask you something?

KAM. Of course.

There is a silence.

AURANGZEB. Am I loveable?

KAM. Father?

AURANGZEB. Are you able to love me?

KAM *kneels and presses his head against his father's hand.*

You look just as I did, boy. I swore that when I became a father I would not have a favourite.

It is clear that KAM *is his favourite.* AURANGZEB *holds him and cries.*

Get out now, boy, leave me, leave.

KAM *takes his leave.* HIRA BAI *sings softly to* AURANGZEB.

Allah was kind when He lent me you, Hira. I must have pleased Him at one time, but then He took you. Would you do something for me, Hira Bai? Would you? Speak to Dara for me. I want to ask him. I want to ask him if he will intercede for me with Allah. I am thirsty, so thirsty.

AURANGZEB *gazes into the light.*

Dara. Just as you said, we were boats dashing together, my darkened eyes did not see your light.

Whatever the wind, brother, I am launching my boat on these waters...

A never-ending ocean without direction.

The End.

Glossary

Ami – mother

Astaghfirullah – I beg forgiveness (from God)

Baba – name for father, both affectionate and honorific

Dargah – Sufi Islamic shrine for a saint. Derived from the Persian word 'portal'

Djinn – spirits with free will, can be good, neutral or malevolent, mentioned in Quran

Hijab – veil worn by women that covers head and chest

Hookah – water pipe with which to smoke flavoured tobacco, fuelled by burning coal

Howdah – carriage on top of an elephant

Imam – Islamic leaders. Lead prayers (Sunni) or are God-chosen community leaders (Shi'a)

Insha'Allah – God willing

Jizya – tax levied on non-Muslims in an Islamic-run state

Mawlana – title given to respected Muslim religious leaders

Muezzin – the person at a mosque who leads the call to prayer

Mullah – title given to a man or woman educated in Islamic theology and sacred law

Salaam – hello, peace

Salaam alaikum – hello to you, peace on you

Salat – the daily prayers of Islam

Qawwali – ancient Sufi devotional music

Wudu – the ritual washing before each prayer

Ya Allah – I need your guidance (from God)

Zakat – tax levied on Muslims in an Islamic-run state

Ajoka Theatre

Ajoka Theatre is Pakistan's leading theatre group committed to 'theatre for social change'. Established in 1984, Ajoka embarked on its journey when the country was being ruled by military dictator General Zia-ul-Haq. Zia had introduced discriminatory 'Islamic' laws, executed popular Prime Minister Zulfiqar Ali Bhutto and banned political activities. Ajoka challenged General Zia's ruthless fundamentalist policies with its bold and innovative plays and performed them all over Pakistan. No auditorium would permit it to perform as the colonial Dramatic Performances Act of 1876 and Martial Law regulations were in use to punish any artists for anti-government art. Ajoka found a safe haven in Lahore's Goethe Institute for several years until civilian rule was restored and the doors of Arts Council auditoriums opened for Ajoka.

Ajoka's repertoire includes major plays on Mughal history such as *Dara*, on Sufi themes such as *Bulha*, about the monumental changes which took place as a result of the Partition of British India including Manto stories and children's play *Border Border*, hard-hitting political satires such as *Burqavaganza* and *America Chalo*, plays on taboo subjects such as blasphemy (*Dekh Tamasha*) and family planning (*Jammanpura*) and plays on violence against women such as *Barri*, *Dukh Darya* and *Kari*.

In Pakistan, Ajoka has been a pioneer in many ways. Firstly, it has established that a socially relevant, quality theatre, which is entertaining as well as educational, is possible in spite of all the political, social and commercial impediments. Secondly, it has linked Pakistan's folk heritage with modern techniques and contemporary content. Thirdly, it has practised a theatre which is modern and not dependent on heavy sets, costumes and other paraphernalia, which has suited contemporary aesthetics and has enabled the group to carry on with limited resources. And fourthly, it has demonstrated that theatre can play a significant role in spreading the message of peace, love and enlightenment even in most difficult political or security situations within the country and the region. Ajoka plays are well known for their bold satires, side-splitting comedies and spectacular storytelling. Usually accompanied by live music, the productions are distinguished by an abundant use of song, dance and festivity. In order to connect with the audiences that are deeply steeped in religious idiom, Ajoka has persistently tried to explore the alternative narratives within Islam such as the culture of Sufism, especially its performative aspects, such as devotional music, qawwali, theatre and dance, all of which celebrate and affirm life.

Ajoka has been actively involved in efforts to promote peace between India and Pakistan through theatre. It has extensively toured India and has performed in places such as Srinagar and Kanyakumari in the south, Kolkatta in the east, and Amritsar in the west. Ajoka has also performed in Oman, Iran, Norway, Bangladesh, Nepal, Hong Kong, Egypt and Britain. It has organised Indo-Pakistan theatre festivals in Lahore and Amritsar, and peace theatre festivals in major cities of Pakistan. Ajoka also publishes books on theatre and produces television plays and documentaries.

Over the past thirty years, Ajoka has become a brand name for Pakistani theatre. Though it is widely admired and appreciated by its audience, irrespective of gender, age, class or creed, it has had its share of adversaries. The regimes have mostly been hostile and suspicious, at best indifferent. Its plays have been banned and its founders have been harassed and persecuted. Ajoka's adaptation of Brecht's *Threepenny Opera* was banned literally at the last minute: the audience found the entrance locked when they came to see the first show. *Burqavaganza* was banned even after the show at the Pakistan National Council of Arts had been publicised and people were queuing up.

Ajoka is led by Shahid Nadeem alongside Founder Artistic Director Madeeha Gauhar, a leading women's rights activist and renowned theatre director, who did her Masters in Theatre Studies at Royal Holloway College, London. She was given the

Tamgha-i-Imtiaz (Medal of Distinction) by the Government of Pakistan in 2003, the Prince Claus Award by the Government of the Netherlands in 2006, the Fatima Jinnah Award by the Government of Pakistan in 2014, and has directed most of Ajoka's plays. Ajoka was given Otto Award for Political Theatre by the Castillo Theater, New York, in 2012.

Ajoka premiered Shahid Nadeem's *Dara* in January 2010 at Alhamra Arts Council, Lahore. Later the play was performed in Karachi and Islamabad. The authorities initially refused permission for performance in Islamabad because they were not ready to approve the script. The matter went to the Senate Committee on Culture where the Minister for Culture accused Ajoka of presenting Dara Shikoh as a hero and Aurangzeb as a villain. Permission was granted only after a heated debate at the Committee and in the media. The play then toured India where it was staged in Amritsar, Delhi, Lucknow, Jaipur and Hyderabad. It was very warmly received in both countries and proved to be an excellent example of promoting peace and goodwill through theatre. The story and message of Prince Dara Shikoh were deliberately ignored by the Pakistani establishment, believers of the 'two nation theory' which had resulted in the Partition of India in 1947. It argued that Aurangzeb, a devout and puritanical Muslim ruler of India who spent most of his forty-year reign unsuccessfully trying to impose Sharia on a predominantly non-Muslim India and fighting rebels in all parts of the Empire, was a role model for the Islamic state of Pakistan, while Prince Dara was just a heretic who had crazy ideas. In India too, Dara's Sufi message has been generally ignored until recently. Ajoka's play was an attempt to correct historical distortions and reclaim Dara, the Sufi, the poet and the scholar of comparative religions, as the role-model Muslim ruler and an icon of Islam, the religion of peace and humanism. Ajoka's *Dara* was also a celebration of the rich Indo-Muslim cultural heritage and a bond which still unites the peoples of India and Pakistan, despite the volatile relations between the two countries.

For more information about Ajoka please visit:
www.ajoka.org.pk

Shahid Nadeem

Shahid Nadeem is an acclaimed Pakistani playwright who has been at the forefront of the campaign for human rights and justice in Pakistan since the late 1960s. Imprisoned by various military regimes and adopted by Amnesty International as a prisoner of conscience, he has been exiled for a period of time. When in exile in London, he worked for Amnesty International as its Campaign Coordinator and Communications Officer. Since his return to Pakistan in the late 1980s, he has served as Executive Director of Ajoka Theatre, Pakistan's leading theatre company, in which capacity he has written, directed and produced plays on a wide range of human-rights themes, including political corruption, gender violence, minority rights, peace and resistance to terrorism. He has written over forty-five plays which have been performed all over Pakistan and India. His adaptations include Brecht's *The Threepenny Opera*, *The Good Person of Szechwan*, *The Resistible Rise of Arturo Ui* and *The Caucasian Chalk Circle*.

Shahid's other plays include:

Bulha: about the life and struggle of the great Sufi poet Bulleh Shah and promoting peace and tolerance.

Aik Thee Naani (*Granny for All Seasons*): about two sisters separated by Partition, highlighting women's right to pursue a career in the performing arts.

Dukh Darya (*River of Sorrow*): based on the true story of a Kashmiri woman who, along with her daughter, became a bone of contention between India and Pakistan, both claimant of the disputed territory of Kashmir.

Barri (*Acquittal*): a play about the anti-women 'Islamic' laws introduced by General Zia-ul-Haq.

Jammanpura (*The Delivery Town*): about the divisive issue of family planning.

Burqavaganza: uses the 'burqa' as a metaphor for religious extremism and hypocrisy in society.

Teesri Dastak (*Third Knock*): about the tenants of a poor tenement threatened with evacuation.

Kala Meda Bhes (*Black are My Robes*): about the struggle for liberation and drinking water by villagers of Cholistan desert.

Dekh Tamasha… (*Watch the Play and Move On*): based on case histories of victims of the controversial Blasphemy Law.

Oxford University Press published a selection of English translations of Shahid's plays under the title *Selected Plays by Shahid Nadeem* in 2008. Seven collections of his plays have been published in Urdu and Punjabi and six in Gurmukhi Punjabi. His plays have been translated into several languages including English. *Aik Thee Naani* (*Granny for All Seasons*) was performed at the Bloomsbury Theatre, London, in 1999. *Bulha* was performed at Riverside Theatre, Hammersmith, in 2006 before touring to Glasgow and Newcastle as part of the Festival of Muslim Cultures. *Barri* (*Acquittal*) was performed at the Highway Theatre, Santa Monica, in 2001. *Burqavaganza* was performed at Brava for Women Theatre in San Francisco, in 2012, under Vidhu Singh's direction. Several of his plays have been given performed readings in various cities around the US. Shahid won the President of Pakistan's Pride of Performance award for literature in 2009.

Shahid was Getty Institute International Scholar and USA's International Pen Visiting International Writer in 2001. It was during this fellowship in Los Angeles that Shahid started research on *Dara,* and some scenes of the play were given a staged reading in Villa Aurora, Los Angeles, in December 2001. He was Democracy Fellow at the National Endowment for Democracy, Washington DC, in 2013–14, where he worked on developing his concept of a Sufi theatre.

Shahid is founder and Executive Director of Ajoka Theatre and also a renowned theatre and television director. He has directed many popular Pakistani TV drama serials and stage plays including *Burqavaganza*, *Hotel Mohenjo Daro*, *Amrika Chalo/Destination USA* and *Dara*. His telefilm *An Act of Terror* received a Scottish BAFTA nomination in 2009 and was screened at London's Asian Film Festival. His documentary on late Bishop John Joseph, *A Sun Sets In*, was selected by South Asian Film Festival for worldwide screening. His telefilm *Mujahid* was screened at the Asia Society, New York, in 2004. He produced documentaries on human rights for Amnesty International in 1991–92. Shahid served on the Pakistan Television Corporation in various capacities including as a producer, general manager, Director of Programmes and Deputy Managing Director. He has been associated with the BBC Urdu Service, with the Pakistani newspapers including *The Herald*, *Newsline* and *Daily Times*, with the Indian magazine, *Frontline*, and with Zee News.

Shahid was born in Sopore, Kashmir. He graduated from the prestigious Government College Lahore and gained his Masters in Applied Psychology from the Punjab University, Lahore. He lives in Lahore, Pakistan, and is married to theatre director Madeeha Gauhar. His daughter Savera and son Nirvaan are well-known actors for Pakistani stage and television.

www.nickhernbooks.co.uk

facebook.com/nickhernbooks

twitter.com/nickhernbooks